60 DAYS OF PRAYER

60 DAYS OF PRAYER

AN INSPIRATIONAL GUIDE FOR PRAYING WITH PURPOSE

Elaine Goddard

ROCKRIDGE PRESS

Copyright © 2021 by Rockridge Press, Oakland, California

No part of this publication may be reproduced, stored in a retrieval system, or transmitted in any form or by any means, electronic, mechanical, photocopying, recording, scanning, or otherwise, except as permitted under Sections 107 or 108 of the 1976 United States Copyright Act, without the prior written permission of the Publisher. Requests to the Publisher for permission should be addressed to the Permissions Department, Rockridge Press, 1955 Broadway, Suite 400, Oakland, CA 94612.

Limit of Liability/Disclaimer of Warranty: The Publisher and the author make no representations or warranties with respect to the accuracy or completeness of the contents of this work and specifically disclaim all warranties, including without limitation warranties of fitness for a particular purpose. No warranty may be created or extended by sales or promotional materials. The advice and strategies contained herein may not be suitable for every situation. This work is sold with the understanding that the Publisher is not engaged in rendering medical, legal, or other professional advice or services. If professional assistance is required, the services of a competent professional person should be sought. Neither the Publisher nor the author shall be liable for damages arising herefrom. The fact that an individual, organization, or website is referred to in this work as a citation and/or potential source of further information does not mean that the author or the Publisher endorses the information the individual, organization, or website may provide or recommendations they/it may make. Further, readers should be aware that websites listed in this work may have changed or disappeared between when this work was written and when it is read.

For general information on our other products and services or to obtain technical support, please contact our Customer Care Department within the United States at (866) 744-2665, or outside the United States at (510) 253-0500.

Rockridge Press publishes its books in a variety of electronic and print formats. Some content that appears in print may not be available in electronic books, and vice versa.

TRADEMARKS: Rockridge Press and the Rockridge Press logo are trademarks or registered trademarks of Callisto Media Inc. and/or its affiliates, in the United States and other countries, and may not be used without written permission. All other trademarks are the property of their respective owners. Rockridge Press is not associated with any product or vendor mentioned in this book.

Interior and Cover Designer: Linda Kocur
Art Producer: Maya Melenchuk
Editor: Brian Sweeting
Production Editor: Dylan Julian
Production Manager: Jose Olivera

All images used under license from Shutterstock
Author photo courtesy of Paige Ramsey, The Ramseys Photography

Unless otherwise noted, scripture quotations are from The Passion Translation®. Copyright © 2017, 2018, 2020 by Passion & Fire Ministries, Inc. Used by permission. All rights reserved. ThePassionTranslation.com.

Scripture quotations marked NIV are from THE HOLY BIBLE, NEW INTERNATIONAL VERSION®, NIV® Copyright © 1973, 1978, 1984, 2011 by Biblica, Inc.® Used by permission. All rights reserved worldwide.

Paperback ISBN: 978-1-63807-076-4 | eBook ISBN: 978-1-63807-865-4
R0

*Dedicated to my LORD, Jesus Christ,
and the family He has given me.*

CONTENTS

Introduction **xii**
How to Use This Book **xiv**

PART ONE:
A (Re)Introduction to Prayer **1**

PART TWO:
60 Days of Prayer **13**

DAY 1:
Adoration: Everything **14**

DAY 2:
Dedication: My Plans **16**

DAY 3:
Supplication: Bold Requests **18**

DAY 4:
Contrition: Statement of Faith and Salvation **20**

DAY 5:
Spiritual Warfare: Putting on Our Protection **22**

DAY 6:
Thanksgiving: Go Out with Joy **24**

DAY 7:
Adoration: Knowing His Name **26**

DAY 8:
Dedication: My Whole Life 28

DAY 9:
Supplication: Intercession
for Family and Friends 30

DAY 10:
Contrition: Forgiveness 32

DAY 11:
Spiritual Warfare: Declaring
Scripture's Promises 34

DAY 12:
Lamenting: Opening to the Holy Spirit 36

DAY 13:
Adoration: Angels in the Throne Room 38

DAY 14:
Dedication: Places 40

DAY 15:
Supplication: Healing Wounds 42

DAY 16:
Contrition: Forgiving Yourself 44

DAY 17:
Spiritual Warfare: Taking Our Position 46

DAY 18:
Centering: Expectant Waiting 48

DAY 19:
Adoration: Jesus Incarnate 50

DAY 20:
Dedication: Our Daily Bread 52

DAY 21:
Supplication: The Lost Sheep **54**

DAY 22:
Contrition: Forgiving God **56**

DAY 23:
Spiritual Warfare: Claiming Our Identity **58**

DAY 24:
Standing: His Promises **60**

DAY 25:
Adoration: His Glory **62**

DAY 26:
Dedication: Our Children **64**

DAY 27:
Supplication: Comfort for Grief **66**

DAY 28:
Contrition: Releasing Resentment **68**

DAY 29:
Spiritual Warfare: Prophetic Intercession **70**

DAY 30:
Resting: Abiding **72**

DAY 31:
Adoration: Stronghold and Refuge **74**

DAY 32:
Dedication: Hope for the Future **76**

DAY 33:
Supplication: His Voice **78**

DAY 34:
Contrition: Surrender **80**

DAY 35:
Spiritual Warfare: Overcoming Shame **82**

DAY 36:
Thanksgiving: Be of Good Cheer **84**

DAY 37:
Adoration: Living Word **86**

DAY 38:
Dedication: My Inner Being **88**

DAY 39:
Supplication: Manifestations of the Spirit **90**

DAY 40:
Contrition: Releasing Pride **92**

DAY 41:
Spiritual Warfare: Overcoming Fear **94**

DAY 42:
Lamenting: A Broken Heart **96**

DAY 43:
Adoration: Our Ascended Lord **98**

DAY 44:
Dedication: Control **100**

DAY 45:
Supplication: Our Nation and Our World **102**

DAY 46:
Contrition: On Behalf of Others **104**

DAY 47:
Spiritual Warfare: Closing Doors **106**

DAY 48:
Centering: Voicing Prayers **108**

DAY 49:
Adoration: The Omni-ness of God 110

DAY 50:
Dedication: My Time 112

DAY 51:
Supplication: Wisdom 114

DAY 52:
Contrition: Repenting on Behalf of My Nation 116

DAY 53:
Spiritual Warfare: Demolishing Strongholds 118

DAY 54:
Standing: Taking Our Post 120

DAY 55:
Adoration: More Than . . . 122

DAY 56:
Dedication: Trust 124

DAY 57:
Supplication: Healing 126

DAY 58:
Contrition: Seventy Times Seven 128

DAY 59:
Spiritual Warfare: Claiming Gates 130

DAY 60:
Resting: It Is Good 132

A Final Word 135
References 136

INTRODUCTION

Prayer is the vehicle to a relationship with our triune God: Father, Son, and Holy Spirit. Often, we pray because it's what we see other believers doing. We pray to follow the commands of scripture or to better know God. While on earth, Jesus lived as the model for praying, so we follow His example.

Learning this interaction with God is much like learning to communicate with our parents as infants. It's okay to be childlike as we cry out to God with a desperate need for help, or to plead for others when their needs are beyond our abilities to satisfy. In this type of praying, we do all the talking. But when we learn to hear what the Father is saying, our dialogue takes on a different dynamic: one of friendship.

God is infinite and able to hear us through the myriad ways we pray. Whether we find ourselves newly on the journey of prayer, struggling with prayer, or longing to dive deeper into prayer, His invitation to get in the vehicle is always open. Moreover, this call is for all followers of Jesus Christ regardless of practice or denomination. In Matthew 6:7, Jesus says, "when you pray," leaving no room for "if." Furthermore, the 1 Thessalonians 5:17–18 instruction to "make your life a prayer" or "pray without ceasing" is distinct no matter the translation.

As a girl, I heard the Lord's invitation to jump into a prayer-filled life. I grew up in a Friends Church (Quaker), where I learned to hear God while sitting in silent Meeting services (or weekly church services). While at a local Baptist church, a mentor introduced me to the power of praying the direct words of scripture. With my family, I learned formal liturgy in the Episcopal church. While working at NASA as an electrical engineer, I deepened my relationship with God and helped others deepen theirs. I completed a master's in biblical life coaching and soul care, have served as a prayer intercessor, and am currently the lay leader of prayer and spirituality at my church. I know the joy of miraculous answers to prayer and the dark nights of grief, family difficulties, injuries, illnesses, and unanswered prayer. My experience is that through every triumph or struggle, the Lord is with me, holding my hand, guiding my footsteps, and ready to save. I love sharing in this psalmist's revelation: "Here's what I've learned through it all: Don't give up; don't be impatient; be entwined as one with the Lord. Be brave and courageous, and never lose hope. Yes, keep on waiting—for he will never disappoint you!" (Psalm 27:14).

HOW TO USE THIS BOOK

Focused on answering the fundamental questions surrounding prayer, part 1 provides an introduction, or a reintroduction, to prayer and its different types. Just one day of people-watching offers ample evidence of our differences. God created us in His image with unique personalities, which logically means God enjoys our individuality. Denominations have been established and built up around prayer styles. Likewise, there are prayer methods named after saints. I hope you will hear God calling in your own voice and style.

Part 2 contains a 60-day prayer devotional. The prayers within the devotional draw you into a specific trajectory of taking the elements of the Lord's Prayer successively deeper.

Each daily entry consists of five parts: a bible verse, a short commentary to unpack the verse's meaning, a reflection to incorporate its lessons into your day, a guided prayer for your practice, and a short breath prayer, which can be used to silently repeat and meditate on throughout your day. Scattered throughout are prayer experiences to assist in transforming our prayers from just the words we say into the lives we live. Since daily practice is vital to strengthening the stronghold of prayer, my recommendation is to complete the devotionals in order. But be encouraged to stop and linger on a specific day, repeating it as you feel is necessary. Likewise, it is perfectly acceptable to enter on the day of a topic of interest. This is a flexible daily devotional, and the devotions may be done on any day of the week. If you miss a day, simply pick up where you stopped and continue.

In addition to setting aside time each day to meet with God, other helpful practices include opening your Bible to linger in the suggested passages, unplugging electronically to avoid distractions, and using a notebook or journal to record your prayers and insights. Furthermore, while praying alone is essential, it is equally important to join others for encouragement and accountability.

PART ONE

A (Re)Introduction to Prayer

__Since most believers testify__ that they pray, does prayer need an introduction? I am confident in the limitlessness of prayer and our need to learn more. In this first section, drawing on scripture, my experiences, and the wisdom of other believers, I will provide principles for understanding God's invitation: the invitation from the Holy One, the Creator of All Things, to commune with Him in this conversation that we call prayer.

What Is Prayer?

I am fascinated by Jesus's words to His disciples in Mark 9:29. When the disciples asked Jesus why they could not cast out the evil spirit, He responded by saying this kind can only come out by prayer. My silent retort on behalf of the disciples goes something like, *Hmm, what do you think we were doing?* Today, Jesus's response is the foundation for my answer to the question, "What is prayer?" Jesus is not referring to the prayer said in the moment of crisis. Jesus is referring to a life and a heart continually drenched in the presence of God. For this to be true, prayer is more than the premeal blessing or church service. Prayer is the very essence of us living out God's presence.

Margaret Therkelsen describes prayer as the great love exchange where we take in the things of God and, having received His love, His character, His creation, respond by loving Him and loving others with His love. Prayer is the deep, living, experiential knowledge of the Triune God. Lacking this type of experiential knowledge often results in prayerlessness.

Is this pragmatic knowing available to you and me, or only to the apostles of scripture, the early Desert Mothers and Fathers who isolated themselves to discover God, the John Wesleys, the Mother Teresas, and the Heidi Bakers? In John 17, Jesus says that He taught about God so that we would know the love that God the Father has for God the Son. In Ephesians 1, Paul calls this experiential knowledge the "hope of his calling." Therefore, assuredly yes, to know and experience the God who dwells within us is for you and me.

Thoughts on Terminology

Different words, including "devotional," "Bible study," "meditation," "petition," and "intercession," may complicate understanding prayer. Devotionals are inspirational stories or Biblical truths that help us know more about God and His interactions with people. They give us hope or increase our faith. However, the prayer devotionals found in the following 60 days are formatted to draw the reader into actively praying.

Bible studies help us learn the scripture, learn about the scripture, and learn about God. In contrast, praying scripture teaches us the language of God. Within the Christian tradition, we meditate on God, scripture, and creation, either for learning about God or hearing from God. The fine line between these purposes of meditation ensures the difficulty of their separation. Meditation to hear God, often referred to as "centering prayer," is explored within the 60 days of prayer. The often-interchangeable use of the words "petition," "intercession," and "prayer" may be confusing. Within the pages of this prayer devotional, both "intercession" and "petition" are included as types of prayers.

The Power of Prayer

The "power of prayer" is a term often heard. There is power in prayer because of the One to whom we pray, not because of our eloquence or level of faith. I received freedom from the fear of praying when, through Francis MacNutt's teachings, I released myself from being responsible for getting answers to prayer. Answers depend on God, and I only need faith to believe that He exists and is able. When we can approach God only to do our part—the asking—we can then stand and watch God do His part: the answering. When we pray, we bridge our physical being, senses, feelings, and thoughts to the Holy Spirit residing within us. This touching of Spirit to flesh can manifest in many ways. 1 Corinthians 12 provides a list of some of the ways we see the unseen Holy Spirit moving. Individual experience with the visible manifestations varies from none to many. God hears, visits, and answers us both with and without physical manifestations.

In my own life, growing up in a Friends church, I confess that many times I left the Meeting unsure of what was being said. Still, in those early Sunday-morning Meetings, God met me, and

I learned to hear His voice within my inner being, and I know that His love surrounded me. In the charismatic services of my college days, I witnessed and experienced many different manifestations of the Holy Spirit. Some left me wondering about their meaning. Even so, God met me there. For me, God meets me with a perception that I can only describe as I know that I know. At times, I see visions. Others experience smells, sounds, and impressions. I had one experience with envisioning holy gold dust. I was sitting in the rehab waiting area, speaking with another stroke recovery patient about hoping in the Lord, when I perceived my left arm to become covered with gold dust. Before my stroke, I would feel what I call Holy Spirit goose bumps on my left arm. However, at the time, my left side affected by the stroke had little to no feeling. So, the Lord gave me gold dust.

Why Pray?

If God is all-knowing, won't He already know our need? And if He's good, won't He provide? It's the great mystery of prayer. Genesis provides insight. God created people in His image and gave us authority on earth—so much power that we could give it away. Because God's holiness couldn't suffer humanity's sinfulness, He became a man—Jesus—to rescue us. And if this is not enough evidence that God chooses to work through people, remember, Jesus prayed.

1 Kings 18:41–19 also shows God waiting to work through prayer. God wanted rain and had Elijah pray for rain. Additionally, in Ezekiel 22:30, God looks for someone who will pray so that He can show His mercy. We come to prayer believing it's our idea, but God initiated prayer to align us with Him and spread His love on earth. Kanita Benson, in her 2021 National Day of Prayer speech, declared this truth: "When the people of God call on the power of God through the authority of God, things change. Every broken place in our nation is a gateway for kingdom advancement and influence, a position for light to penetrate darkness." When we pray, we're

not trying to manipulate God into doing what we want. Praying helps us surrender and lay hold of our loving God's promises.

While it is God's design to bring us into a relationship with Him to spread His love, we come to prayer for some of the following reasons as individuals.

We Pray Because We Need God

We come to prayer either out of total surrender from a place we can't fix from within ourselves, or we enter into conversation with God to remind ourselves that we need God. Prayer writes "God is God, and I am not" on our hearts and minds.

We Pray for Companionship

God created us because He wanted fellowship. Being made in His image, we have a giant hole within our inner being that longs for connection. Prayer fills our void of loneliness. We come to God when we feel alone in the darkness of the night.

We Pray for Wholeness

Unable to solve the physical and mental needs around us, we fall to our knees and cry out. Whether for ourselves, for loved ones, or the plight of the world, we need the One who is more incredible than ourselves to heal, restore, and redeem.

We Pray Because It Is Commanded

While many turn away from the "because I said so" argument, those of us with rule-following personalities need to know that God's word calls us to be people of prayer. In Matthew 6, Jesus begins His teachings on prayer with "when you pray." He starts teaching with the assumption that prayer is already done. Additionally, in 1 Thessalonians 5:16–18, we are instructed that to pray without ceasing is God's will for us. As homes for the living God, our name is house of prayer.

Summary

From Adam's first breath through eternity, God is wooing us and longing for us to meet with Him. He wants to love us, for us to receive His love, and for us to spread His love to others. Richard J. Foster in *Finding the Heart's True Home* sums up the answer to what draws us to pray: "The truth of the matter is, we all come to prayer with a tangled mass of motives altruistic and selfish, merciful and hateful, loving and bitter. Frankly, this side of eternity we will never unravel the good from the bad, the pure from the impure. God is big enough to receive us with all our mixture." And that is the good news: God receives us as we are, He likes who we are, and He enjoys us.

Types of Prayer

Scripture declares that there is more than one form or type of prayer: "Pray passionately in the Spirit, as you constantly intercede with every form of prayer at all times. Pray the blessings of God upon all his believers" (Ephesians 6:18). People have been labeling prayer since the first account of prayer. Numerous kinds, styles, classes, and forms of prayer exist. Entering the words "types of prayer" into Google will bring over 100 million results, each containing a list of varying numbers and labels. And these prayers may be said alone or communally, silently or out loud. Prayers may be prayed while standing, sitting, kneeling, dancing, breathing, with coffee, at home, at church, at the park, at the office, and in the grocery store. We often limit our encounters with God, searching for the perfect time, place, and way. Attempting to become subject matter experts, we study prayer like a classroom subject. Prayer, however, is to be enjoyed as we daily experience life.

Joining into this array of lists, I have endeavored to make one of my own. The first five types are the elements of the Lord's Prayer from Matthew 6:9–13. The remainder of the list are styles that will be encountered in the following prayer devotional.

Elements of the Lord's Prayer

Beginning with the familiar words of the prayer that Jesus taught, the first five types of prayer will be repeated throughout the devotional, with each succession taking a step further into our connection with the Lord.

> *This, then, is how you should pray: "Our Father in heaven, hallowed be your name, your kingdom come, your will be done, on earth as it is in heaven. Give us today our daily bread. And forgive us our debts, as we also have forgiven our debtors. And lead us not into temptation, but deliver us from the evil one."*
> —MATTHEW 6:9–13 (NIV)

Adoration: "Hallowed be your name"

In Isaiah's vision of God's heavenly throne room, the Seraphim cries, "Holy!" (Isaiah 6:3). As we make declarations of God's glory, our eyes are lifted heavenward, focused on our King. As we declare the glory of His character through His revealed names, we grow into a deeper understanding of who He is. Praising God for who He is transforms our attitudes to become aligned with heaven and invites us into God's presence and God into our presence.

Dedication: "Your kingdom come, your will be done"

These are prayers of consecration or surrender. In petitions of sacrifice, we release control of our thoughts, actions, and plans to the Lord. We move out of our kingdom of self into the kingdom of God. In addition to ourselves, we dedicate our finances, our things, and our loved ones to the Lord. Do not fear; I will not be asking for your money but leading you in entreaties of surrender that ask God for His direction and wisdom over our resources and things.

Supplication: "Give us today our daily bread"

These are prayers of petition and intercession where we ask for our needs, and we intercede for the needs of others. We call upon the mercy, grace, and power of God to provide, heal, redeem, and restore ourselves, loved ones, community, state, nation, and world. We knock, and we keep knocking. Instead of bringing our complaint, we sit with scripture and pray in alignment with how Jesus is mediating for us from heaven.

Contrition: "Forgive us our debts, as we also have forgiven our debtors"

We humbly come before the Lord and confess when we haven't done what we should, or we have done what we shouldn't. We call upon his promises and his mercy and ask Him to forgive us. We ask for His understanding and love to flow through us so that we can forgive others.

Spiritual Warfare, Deliverance: "Lead us not into temptation, but deliver us from the evil one"

While we cannot ignore the spiritual battle that rages around us, the good news is that God has granted us the tools and the authority to stand against Satan and the rulers of darkness that come against us. Within spiritual warfare prayers, we put on our protection, shine His light, and declare the hope, redemption, and freedom that Jesus offers.

Experiential Prayer Styles

After each successive walk through the elements of the Lord's Prayer, the prayer devotional will contain a prayer experience. Prayer experiences are styles of praying that take us away from our coffee and comfy chair. They envelop us within the loving presence of God as we go about our daily activities. These prayer styles aid the transference of prayer from a matter of thought—practicing a discipline—to a matter of heart—responding to love.

Thanksgiving

While worship and adoration acknowledge God for who He is, thanksgiving acknowledges God for what He has done. More than the premeal blessing, we give God the glory and credit for His works around us, His works through us, and His works for us. The Protestant tradition adds a line of praise to the end of the Lord's Prayer.

Lamenting

In prayers of lament, we allow God to open our eyes, our hearts, and our minds to see as He sees and to experience the gap between how things are and how He longs for them to be. We allow the Holy

Spirit to break our hearts for what breaks His, and we weep before the Lord, crying out to Him in the anguish of our spirit.

Centering

In centering prayer, we calm our physical being to rest in the quiet awareness of God's presence. This method allows us to clear our minds of the clutter of the world and focus on God. During the time of prayer, we consent to God's presence and action within. At other times our attention moves outward to discover God's presence all around.

Standing

Standing and watching can be a challenging form of prayer. Most of us desire to be in action and fix the problem. Scripture calls us to watch, and stand in victory. Listening to the Lord and understanding when we are to stop and stand is essential.

Resting

Even harder than standing is resting. After God completed creation, He rested, and He calls us to experience His rest. In our entertainment-driven world, we view resting as being fascinated by something or engaged in something. God's call is to rest in Him under the shadow of His wings.

Breath Prayers

Breath prayers (said in one breath) are short phrases of praise, petition, intercession, or declaration. Breath prayers help build a prayer-filled life that answers the call to pray without ceasing. Each day of the following 60-day prayer devotional will end with a suggested breath prayer for you to write on your heart and breath until time for the subsequent devotional.

TIPS FOR DEVELOPING A STRONG PRAYER PRACTICE

To pray with purpose is to follow the greatest commandments of loving God with our whole heart and loving our neighbors as ourselves. Through the following prayer devotional, you will enter into the journey of engaging God to receive His love for yourself and others. Each day of this devotional invites you into prayer with an idea and sample prayer or prayer activity that is a place to start. View these prayer devotionals as launching platforms for your continued conversation with God the Father, God the Son, and God the Holy Spirit.

- Pray with an open Bible, having God's word available for meditation, reflection, and guidance.

- Record prayers.

- Record answers to prayers.

- Record experiences during prayer.

- Set aside time to pray.

- Have a piece of paper and pen ready to record everything that enters your mind as a distraction. Writing it down will release your mind from dwelling on it.

- Set the environment and try different settings: quiet, with music, inside, outside, etc.

- Unplug, removing distractions from electronic communication and social media.

- Partner with two or three others to experience the 60-day prayer devotional together. This partnership is for both encouragement and accountability.

PART TWO

60 Days of Prayer

In books, blogs, and podcasts, *society talks a lot about prayer. Conversely, when Jesus is asked how to pray, He responds with the 57-word Lord's Prayer, and communing with God is its purpose. In this section, you'll pray using the Lord's Prayer as your guide. After my stroke, as I relearned how to walk, my physical therapists repeatedly told me, "You have to walk to walk." Not by thinking about it—I had to walk in order to walk. Likewise, you have to pray to pray. May this section lead you to a closer relationship with God the Father, Son, and Spirit.*

DAY

1

Adoration: Everything

With my whole heart, with my whole life, and with my innermost being, I bow in wonder and love before you, the holy God!
—PSALM 103:1 (TPT)

The first petition of the Lord's Prayer is to adore God. David, in Psalm 103, says that our adoration involves more than our voice. Praise to our holy God should include everything. When there is poor execution of a task, we recognize it as half-hearted. It is easy to only give our voice to praise God. And while it is challenging to gauge the sincerity of praise, I can judge the amount of time I devote to glorifying God. Even setting the goal of praising God for five minutes a day can positively impact our outlook for the entire day. If you are like me, it can feel overwhelming to think about all the areas of our lives that need prayer. But by aligning our lives with heaven, our whole lives can be an act of praise.

REFLECT

- In addition to using words, how else do you praise God? "Break forth with dancing! Make music and sing God's praises with the rhythm of drums!" (Psalm 149:3).
- Set a practical step goal for moving from how much you praise God now toward unending praise. For example, if you currently praise God one day a week, set a goal to praise Him three days a week. Or if you glorify Him two times a day, increase that to three times a day.

Pray

Set a length of time from 5 to 30 minutes and pick an activity in which you actively praise the Lord.

Possible activities include singing, dancing, playing an instrument, writing God a letter of praise, drawing, or painting your impression of a psalm. Begin your activity with a prayer. If you become distracted during your time of praise, use your breath prayer to regain focus on devotion to the Lord.

Father, I come before you with all that I am and praise You with _____
(your selected activity)

HOLY IS THE LORD!

DAY 2

Dedication: My Plans

So above all, constantly seek God's kingdom and his righteousness, then all these less important things will be given to you abundantly.
—MATTHEW 6:33 (TPT)

The familiar words of Matthew 6:10 (NIV), "your kingdom come, your will be done," hide our role in living this petition. Until Jesus returns, we're the kingdom's light-bringers to the world. Accepting Christ as our Savior means we take Him as Lord of our life. But do we repeat this petition without giving thought to surrendering our plans to God? Many may not even be sure that they want to be the kingdom's light-bringers. Others fear that surrendering to the Lordship of Jesus will remove all evidence of joy from their lives. In Matthew 5:14–16, Jesus says that our very lives light up the world and that we are to shine.

As written in the New American Standard Bible, this verse was one of the first scripture prayers that the Holy Spirit taught me to pray. I felt His call but wasn't sure I wanted to be an intercessor. As I prayed these powerful words over myself, my spirit recognized several things. For the first time, I had complete and total confidence that I was asking something that I knew was God's will for me and anyone I prayed for using these words of scripture. Additionally, as I prayed these words over myself each morning, they came true. I could not wait to seek Him out each day. I loved my time in His word and learning more about Him. I started finding Him in the words of scripture.

REFLECT

- Looking at your day, what gets most of your time?
- What does it mean to seek after God's kingdom?
- How do you seek His kingdom?

Pray

It is okay to be hesitant. Giving up our perceived control is difficult. Share with God where you are today. Ask Him for help to just say the words.

Lord Jesus, I'm not sure what putting Your kingdom first means, and I'm not sure I would want to lay down my plans and dreams of _____ if You were to ask me to. I ask You to give me the heart to put You above anything else and to grant me the ability to be Your kingdom's light in all that I think, say, and do. Amen.

I SEEK GOD.

DAY

3

Supplication: Bold Requests

You jealously want what others have so you begin to see yourself as better than others. You scheme with envy and harm others to selfishly obtain what you crave—that's why you quarrel and fight. And all the time you don't obtain what you want because you won't ask God for it!
—JAMES 4:2 (TPT)

I am astounded by the number of times my husband and I discovered after an event that one of our kids wanted to participate. We found out that reason they didn't ask was that they assumed the answer would be no. Sometimes the answer may have been yes, but it was always no simply because they never asked. Many of us approach God in the same manner. We do not ask for the specific things we need and want out of an assumption God won't answer, or that if He does, His answer will be no. Equally wrong is the notion of not asking because we view asking for help as a lower form of prayer. Yet Jesus Himself instructs us to ask. Not only does He tell us to ask in the Lord's Prayer, but also throughout the Gospel, as in John 16:24: "Until now you've not been bold enough to ask the Father for a single thing in my name, but now you can ask, and keep on asking him! And you can be sure that you'll receive what you ask for, and your joy will have no limits!" And lastly, we do not ask out of feelings of unworthiness or shame. God sent us His son, Jesus, to show us His love, and He calls us His children fully adopted into His family.

REFLECT

What holds you back from making your requests to God?

Pray

James tells us that there is a better way. In place of jealously scheming, ask God. And Jesus says to be bold in our requests. Today, using any of the following prayer models, come to the Father and share your dreams, desires, and needs.

Dear heavenly Father, I lay before You my dream of _____. And ask that you bring it to be. In the name of Jesus, amen.

God, here I am once again asking that You will provide _____. In the name of Jesus, amen.

God in heaven, I know You know my needs and desires. I ask You to _____. In the name of Jesus, amen.

GOD, I ASK.

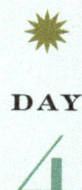

DAY

4

Contrition: Statement of Faith and Salvation

For here is the way God loved the world—he gave his only, unique Son as a gift. So now everyone who believes in him will never perish but experience everlasting life. God did not send his Son into the world to judge and condemn the world, but to be its Savior and rescue it!
—JOHN 3:16–17 (TPT)

The beauty of Christianity is that our salvation is free. It can't be earned. There is no works program, and there is no measuring rod of goodness required to obtain admittance. Even after completing this prayer devotional, God won't love you more than He does now. God has already provided the way and longs for us to enter into it. The first step is recognizing that we need saving and believe that Jesus Christ has already saved us. Our acceptance of the grace, extended to everyone through the passion and sacrifice of Jesus Christ, is what makes us worthy to enter the family of God. As such, God sees our needs, our pits, our devastations, and He answers our cry for help.

REFLECT

- What do you consider your inheritance?
- What do you believe you deserve or have earned?

Pray

There are many prayers and prayer models to express our desire for salvation and our profession of faith. Scripture says to believe and receive. I have provided a simple prayer of salvation and my prayer declaring my faith. Pray these prayers or write out one of your own.

Salvation: Father in heaven, I am a sinner, I have done _____, and do not deserve Your love. I accept and receive Your freely offered gift of mercy obtained through the sacrifice of Jesus Christ.

Faith: God, You are the most high God, creator of all things. By the pure and holy blood of Your Son, my Lord Jesus Christ, I am a blessed, loved, adopted, chosen, redeemed, child of God who is sealed by the Holy Spirit. Through Your Holy Spirit, I will hear Your voice, and I will follow You, to whatever end, no matter the cost.

LORD, MY PORTION.

DAY 5

Spiritual Warfare: Putting on Our Protection

> *Put on God's complete set of armor provided for us so that you will be protected as you fight against the evil strategies of the accuser!*
> —EPHESIANS 6:11 (TPT)

Many believe spiritual warfare is unnecessary because God has already defeated evil. Yes, we know the ending that God wins! However, the evil one still desires to take us out. But we shouldn't live in fear, for God gave us authority in the battle (Luke 10:19). Hiding isn't enough. As Aragorn said to King Théoden in *The Lord of the Rings: The Two Towers*, open war is at our borders. One time, an exterminator entered our house. Unprompted, he told me that he'd been calling people from church, asking to pray. But the last few evenings, as he'd prepared to make the calls, he'd become violently ill. When he gave up trying, the illness passed. I asked if he'd first put on the armor of God, and he defensively responded, "I am a

Christian." I said, "The armor *is* for believers," and recited Ephesians 6:13: "You must wear all the armor that God provides so you're protected as you confront the slanderer, for you are destined for all things and will rise victorious." The liar will stop at nothing to keep us from praying with purpose and power. Before we pray or live our day, we should put on the protection that God has provided.

REFLECT

Do you know the elements of the armor of God (belt of truth, breastplate of righteousness, shoes of the gospel of peace, shield of faith, sword of the spirit, helmet of salvation) and the protection each one provides?

Pray

Holy Father, I walk in Your protection. I put on truth. Father, forgive me for allowing lies and falsehoods from slipping out of my mouth. Give me strength to speak the truth and Your words of truth. I put on the righteousness of Your son, Jesus Christ. Guard my heart with Your love and mercy. I pick up my shield of faith and trust in You. Lord, strengthen my grip, for this shield can extinguish every fiery arrow the enemy sends toward me. And I take with me Your word, the sword of Your Spirit. Through the power of Jesus's name, amen.

LORD, MY PROTECTION.

DAY 6

Thanksgiving: Go Out with Joy

For the kingdom of God is not a matter of rules about food and drink, but is in the realm of the Holy Spirit, filled with righteousness, peace, and joy.
—ROMANS 14:17 (TPT)

One day at the dinner table, I asked my teenage daughters if being a Christian was fun. They were very skeptical of the notion that Christianity was fun. As they argued against this idea, one of them said, "Unless you are Alexis from youth group." They all agreed, saying, "The joy of the Lord just spills from her. She looks like she's having fun." What a beautiful description of going out with joy; it unfortunately doesn't apply to every follower. Isaiah 55:12 reads, "Go out with joy" (NIV). Yes, we must lay our troubles at the cross and go out with joy.

When we're focused on the trouble of our world, we don't give our hearts space for rejoicing. Yet, scripture commands we be joyful. The joy of the Lord can't be faked but can be practiced.

Today, we practice overflowing joy by thanking God for all He's done. Throughout the Old Testament, God tells people to set a stone or build an altar so that they would remember. He knows our memory is fleeting, causing a lack of joy. To combat this, my family places rocks in a basket to mark significant events.

REFLECT

- What percentage of your day are you joyful?
- How can you increase that percentage?

Pray

One method for practicing walking in overflowing joy is to thank the Lord. Since today is a prayer experience of thanksgiving, we will pause at every doorframe and give the Lord anything that is causing us to be negative, angry, resentful, or bitter. Then we are going to replace that thought or emotion by thanking God for something He has done. You can thank Him for something recent or from long ago. As you leave the doorframe, breathe your breath prayer, "I choose joy." Before you start, say a prayer asking God to bring to your remembrance things that He has done for you.

Holy Father, I ask that You replay before my mind's eye all that You have done on my behalf. Amen.

I CHOOSE JOY.

DAY 7

Adoration: Knowing His Name

God said to Moses, "I am who I am."
—EXODUS 3:14A (NIV)

In Matthew 6:9, Jesus teaches prayer, beginning with "Our Beloved Father, dwelling in the heavenly realms, may the glory of your name be the center on which our lives turn" (TPT). Declaring God's existence may seem simple, like it doesn't need mentioning. However, God declares God: "I Am," the essential truth that God exists. God reveals that He is self-existent, self-evidencing, self-giving, self-directed, unchanging, and present with this statement. And the mere fact that He *is* should be the drive of the rest of our lives.

For God to be the focus of our life, we need to know His name and understand its meaning. God tells us His names to reveal His character. The first name He reveals to us is "I Am." Believing that God is, has always been, and will always be is our first step to coming before Him.

This belief is the tiny mustard seed of faith that will grow into the mature tree when nurtured. In John 8:24, Jesus also claims this name, saying, "I Am who I Am." Our response to knowing God independently exists is to worship Him. This is exemplified by Job when he falls before the Lord and declares, "You are God and I am not." Likewise, King David affirms this worship response in Psalm 139:2: "I bow down before your divine presence and bring you my deepest worship as I experience your tender love and your living truth. For your Word and the fame of your name have been magnified above all else!"

REFLECT

- Why is it revolutionary for God to tell Moses that His name is "I Am"?
- What is the importance of calling someone by name?

Pray

Yahweh, You are holy, the great I Am. You are the uncreated, creating God, and I lift Your name on high. May all the earth join in with my shouts of praise to You. Yahweh, the blessed one, who was, who is, and who will be, holy are You.

HOLY YAHWEH.

DAY 8

Dedication: My Whole Life

> *I heard your voice in my heart say, "Come, seek my face;" my inner being responded, "Yahweh, I'm seeking your face with all my heart."*
> —PSALM 27:8 (TPT)

Some have said Jesus's prayer so often that the full impact of its meaning no longer penetrates their core. "Your will be done" are words of surrender. When we accept Jesus as Savior, we're granted peace with God. To live in this peace, we must respond to the Holy Spirit that says, "Seek God's face." David expresses this total surrender in the poetic language of Psalm 27:4. "Here's the one thing I crave from Yahweh, the one thing I seek above all else: I want to live with him every moment in his house, beholding the marvelous beauty of Yahweh." David wrote this long before a temple had been built. He was professing his desire to be in God's presence.

Another reason we struggle with surrender is fear. We come to God afraid. We're fearful of what He will ask us to do. We don't realize that the first place of surrender is allowing Him to reveal the hope of His calling (Ephesians 1:18). Instead of worrying about what we should do and who we should be, He asks us to do and be with Him. Sometimes this is a significant career change or focus, and sometimes this is a nudge to be with Him right where you are.

REFLECT

- Based on how you spend your time, who or what is your one thing?
- Who or what do you desire to be your one thing?

Pray

This prayer releases complete control of ourselves to the one who created us. God is the one who formed and shaped us in our mother's wombs (Psalm 139:13).

Holy Father, I think I want the words "surrender all" to be true of me. I confess I have made my own life plans. Holy Spirit, open my ears to you. Respond from deep within me to seek God's face. In the holy name of Jesus, amen.

Holy Father, I declare that You are my one thing. I trade my kingdom and glory for Yours. May I walk in Your presence all my days. In Jesus's name, amen.

YOU ARE MY ONE THING.

DAY 9

Supplication: Intercession for Family and Friends

> *Most of all, I'm writing to encourage you to pray with gratitude to God. Pray for all men with all forms of prayers and requests as you intercede with intense passion.*
> —1 TIMOTHY 2:1 (TPT)

Notice that the Lord's Prayer is communal in all its petitions: "Our Father," "our daily bread." Jesus calls us to look beyond our own needs to our collective needs. This verse is the foundation for my coaching of interpreting scripture when we intercede for others. They are rose-colored by the redeeming blood of Christ Jesus. We come to God with gratitude. If our heart is not in the place to be grateful for the person directly, then we come thankful for God. The next step is often the hardest. We do not list their circumstances, decisions, attitudes, and so on, for God sees and already knows. As long as we air our complaints before God, we are not interceding, and our hearts and minds, while full of emotion, are earth-focused. To intercede, we put on the mind of Christ, and as Oswald Chambers says, we put ourselves in God's place, having His mind and perspective.

REFLECT

- How do you pray for your loved ones?
- Do you pray with gratitude or begrudgingly?

Pray

Sitting with the wisdom of scripture aligns our hearts with God's plans and purposes. As long as we are detailing the circumstances, we are not praying, and possibly even worse, we align with the accuser of the brethren (Revelation 12:10). Additionally, moving straight to praying in a communal prayer setting prevents the gathering from disintegrating into a gossip session.

After reading 1 Timothy 2:1, pray the following prayer over the first names that come into your mind.

Glorious Father, transform _____'s heart to examine what _____ does by how _____ does it. That _____ may grow in desire to do everything in love. Through Jesus Christ who loved _____ first, amen.

LOVE AS GOD LOVES.

DAY 10

Contrition: Forgiveness

Forgive us the wrongs we have done as we ourselves release forgiveness to those who have wronged us.
—MATTHEW 6:12 (TPT)

I was a young teen saying this line of the prayer that Jesus taught his disciples when my voice caught, and understanding of the true meaning of this phrase flooded my entire being. In praying Matthew 6:12, I was asking God to forgive me just like I forgave others. Throughout the Gospel, Jesus teaches the importance of forgiving one another to receive our Father's forgiveness. He illustrates this concept in the parable of the unmerciful servant found in Matthew 18:21–35. And in Mark 11:25–26, He instructs us to stop praying and forgive others before continuing to pray. Whether navigating the difficulties of mean girls, family, road rage, racial tension, offense, or hate, we are to walk in His way of forgiveness (Romans 5:8). Jesus desires for us to both seek and release God's love and compassion. Throughout scripture, there are no exemptions; we are to forgive as

God forgives us so that God can forgive us as we forgive others.

REFLECT

- What holds you back from asking for God's forgiveness?
- Do you feel you can't forgive yourself?
- What holds you back from forgiving others?

Pray

As believers in Christ Jesus, we have already received the gift of mercy when we accepted Christ as our Lord and Savior. For more information, refer to the prayer for salvation from day 4. Today's prayer of forgiveness, as modeled below, keeps us in relationship with our heavenly Father. In this invocation, we ask God for forgiveness, permit Him to search our inner being (Psalm 139), and ask for His strength to break open the dam within our hearts, thereby releasing the flow of His mercy through us to others.

Dear God, I was wrong. I sinned against You when I (did/said/didn't do/thought) _____. Please forgive me. Please forgive me for not loving _____ as You love _____. God, I ask for Your strength to release Your grace and mercy to _____ so that I can say, "I forgive _____ for _____ and to no longer hold _____ against them." In Jesus's name, amen.

MERCIFUL LORD.

DAY

11

Spiritual Warfare: Declaring Scripture's Promises

So also will be the word that I speak; it does not return to me unfulfilled. My word performs my purpose and fulfills the mission I sent it out to accomplish."
—ISAIAH 55:11 (TPT)

Words, once spoken, are forever heard and repeated. Scripture tells us that our words have the power of life and death (Proverbs 18:21). God spoke creation into being, and He declares in Isaiah 55:11 that His word accomplishes the purposes He has for it. When we pray God's direct words aloud, we tap into the creation power that He gave us (2 Corinthians 4:7). When we pray according to God's word, we're aligned with His heart. The evil one comes to kill, steal, and destroy. He speaks lies to us to break our trust in God. Using words for life can transform hearts.

When I taught at prayer conference, the atmosphere was of doubt and fear. This group, as individuals, hardly opened their Bibles. I asked them to underline a passage of scripture and then write it out as a prayer. All their pushback as to why they couldn't pray the words of scripture came against me like a physical force. Prompted by the Holy Spirit, I began praying out loud the words of the selected scripture. As I prayed over each one of them by name, the spoken word of God changed the atmosphere in the room, and it changed not only their hearts but also my heart.

REFLECT

- What words do you speak in your mind to yourself?
- What words do you speak out loud to yourself and others?
- Do your words bring life?

Pray

While God does not promise lack of difficulty or trouble, God promises His faithful grace to endure or the grace of escape. Pray the following promises of God's word out loud and declare them as true for yourself and your family.

God's word is truth (John 17:17). God is good (Psalm 100:5). I am a child of God (John 1:12).

YES AND AMEN.

DAY 12

Lamenting: Opening to the Holy Spirit

... Holy Spirit rises up within us to super-intercede on our behalf, pleading to God with emotional sighs too deep for words.
—ROMANS 8:26 (TPT)

It's okay not to know how to pray. I once led a small team as we prayed over a young mother. She presented her request for healing with a brave voice and a smile. When we asked the Holy Spirit how to proceed, He broke our hearts with His love for her, and we all wept. Our outward weeping was against the procedures we'd been taught. However, God had His way, as the Spirit within her connected to the Holy Spirit within the team, and we pleaded to God on her behalf through tears and groans. I watched a single tear roll down her cheek. She said that she hadn't allowed tears to flow over, trying to be a strong mother. However, that afternoon the team climbed up on the ash heap (Job 2) with her and let the Holy Spirit weep. She poured out her questions, her angst against God, and her fears, grief, and despair. In that release, the Holy Spirit restored her hope.

When we allow the Holy Spirit to lament through us, the Lord's healing is released. Intercessions of lament strengthen our souls. It's a deep inner groan over what breaks God's heart. While some individuals are gifted in lamenting, all can be trained. The key is to be willing to open our eyes, ears, and hearts and allow the Holy Spirit to intercede through us.

REFLECT

- How do you feel about weeping as prayer?
- Are you willing to allow the Holy Spirit to pray through you?

Pray

Pick an area that you have been soldiering through. The possibilities are endless and can be a sickness, a family conflict, or a brokenness in your city or nation. Come to the Lord and confess you do not know what to do. Freely make your accusations, bring Him your questions, and ask Him to give you His eyes to see, His ears to hear, and His heart to grieve. Allow the groans and sighs of the Holy Spirit to pour through your whole being. Sit with the Holy Spirit on the ash heap and experience the devastation of this broken world and His desire for it to be whole.

LORD, BREAK MY HEART.

DAY 13

Adoration: Angels in the Throne Room

And one called out to another, saying: "Holy, holy, holy is the Lord God, Commander of Angel Armies! The whole earth is filled with his glory!"
—ISAIAH 6:3 (TPT)

As we walk this earth, watch the news, and hear of destruction and trouble, we become filled with the devastation of this broken world. The Seraphim of Isaiah 6:3, however, only see the glory of God. And they declare that His glory fills the earth. I believe this is the type of true worship on which the world groans in wait (Romans 8). Worship that sees the glory of God not as something far off in heaven or far off in the awaited future, but the glory that currently fills the earth. The glory of God resides in us as His sons and daughters. To worship with angels in heaven's throne room, we must burn with adoration for the living God.

How do we enter the throne room? Read Isaiah 6:6–7. Isaiah recognized that he could not declare the glory of the Lord with the same lips that were tainted with sin. The angel of his vision took a burning coal from the altar, touched his lips, and declared that his guilt was removed. The mercy sacrifice of Jesus Christ covers us as believers. We stand before the throne of God clothed in the righteousness of Jesus Christ.

REFLECT

- What does it mean for your heart to burn with adoration?
- Why do you think the Seraphim repeat the word "holy" three times?
- How is it possible to declare the glory of the Lord with the same lips and voice that sin?

Pray

This is a prayer of visualization. Begin this prayer by confessing and receiving the forgiveness of God. Then boldly enter into the throne room of the almighty God. See the Seraphim with their six wings, feel the thunderousness of their voices, and hear their words. Join in with the Seraphim and declare, "Holy, holy, holy is the Lord God almighty! Holy, holy, holy is the Lord God almighty! Holy, holy, holy is the Lord God almighty!"

Holy Spirit, grant that my heart burn with singular adoration of God. Through the work of Christ Jesus, amen.

HOLY ARE YOU, LORD!

DAY 14

Dedication: Places

If God's grace doesn't help the builders, they will labor in vain to build a house. If God's mercy doesn't protect the city, all the sentries will circle it in vain.
—PSALM 127:1 (TPT)

Throughout the Old Testament, when the Israelites moved to a new location, they often built an altar and dedicated it to the Lord. While there are no specific instructions to devote our homes and businesses to God within scripture, this is a practical extension of surrendering. We hand over our kingdoms in the form of our homes, businesses, and communities to God for His kingdom glory. Proverbs 24:3–4 tells us that when builders of these things build with wisdom, hearts are filled with the pleasures of spiritual wealth.

Many people actively join in dedicating church buildings and church grounds to the Lord, but how many of us surrender the places that we spend most of our time? Prayers of dedication announce to our hearts and to God that this place, this land, this home, or this business is God's for His purpose and His kingdom glory. With this stance, we not only ask for the Lord's protection from evil, but we are also announcing our commitment to actively participate in protecting it from evil influences.

REFLECT

- What types of activities take place within your home and business?
- Do you actively take a stand against evil influences within your home?
- How do you take a stand without it becoming a legalistic list of dos and don'ts?

Pray

Holy Father, fixing my eyes on Jesus, I give You this _____ to be used for Your plans and purposes. Open my eyes to how I may participate in using this _____ for Your glory. Amen.

ALL I HAVE IS YOURS.

DAY 15

Supplication: Healing Wounds

He heals the wounds of every shattered heart.
—PSALM 147:3 (TPT)

In Luke 4, Jesus proclaims that He is the fulfillment of this scripture of Isaiah 61:1, which says: "Yahweh sent me to heal the wounds of the brokenhearted, to tell captives, 'You are free,' and to tell prisoners, 'Be free from your darkness.'" This is Jesus's mission statement. Since Jesus says this is who He is, we can be assured that praying for our healing is God's will.

Unfortunately, we tend to listen to the enemy's lies and allow old wounds to block the healing that Jesus offers. Doubt, disgrace, lost hope, and other symptoms of a wounded heart often take longer and more effort to heal than physical injury. In our world of instant gratification, we often give up before wholeness occurs. When my college prayer group learned of the brutal attack on another student named Wendy, we prayed for her. I wrote her name next to scripture I prayed for her, and every Sunday group gathering for two years, we prayed

Isaiah 62:1–5 over Wendy. Later, whenever I saw her name in my Bible, I'd say another prayer. Twenty-eight years after I first wrote "Wendy 1986" in the margin of my Bible, she was speaking at a conference I attended. Wendy tells her story in her book *Hidden Joy in a Dark Corner: The Transforming Power of God's Story.*

It is an honor to know that God called me to join Him in the call for her healing. This is the authority and power that the Lord has given to His people. God answers your prayers.

REFLECT

- How long have you prayed for something or someone?
- Are you still praying for the issue? If not, why not?

Pray

God, for _____'s sake I will not keep silent, and for their soul I will not keep quiet, until _____'s righteousness goes forth like brightness, and _____'s salvation is like a torch that is burning. But _____ will be called "My delight is in them," and to Jesus they will be covenanted, and as the bridegroom rejoices over the bride, so God will rejoice over _____, and they will receive His joy.

JEHOVAH-RAPHA (THE LORD WHO HEALS).

DAY 16

Contrition: Forgiving Yourself

But instead be kind and affectionate toward one another. Has God graciously forgiven you? Then graciously forgive one another in the depths of Christ's love.
—EPHESIANS 4:32 (TPT)

The concept of self-forgiveness is not directly addressed within the pages of scripture. But Christ tells us that the second-greatest command is to love others as we love ourselves. However, some of us may not love others very well because we may not love ourselves. We have not allowed the redeeming love of God to wash away our sin, shame, and doubt. Two of the most common reasons why are: First, we put ourselves in a spiritual time-out from God because of what we have or haven't done. And second, we have asked for His forgiveness for an issue but have not believed we have received it, so we repeatedly ask. In the first case, we are putting ourselves in the position of God and making judgments over ourselves. In the second case, we are not trusting that God is who He says He is. This lack of trust is a lack of faith in God.

By not receiving the love and grace of God's forgiveness as available for ourselves, we miss out on God's rest. Often this results in self-destruction by our own thought life. Your mind can't tell the difference between false and true guilt triggers. Both will make you feel miserable and weak. The Bible says that we love because He first loved us (1 John 4:9). To love and forgive ourselves, we must fully receive within our inner being the love and forgiveness of God.

REFLECT

- What holds you back from receiving the forgiveness of God?
- Do you need to seek forgiveness from someone?
- Do you need to forgive someone?

Pray

The Lord is still waiting to show His favor to me. Lord, show me Your marvelous love. Lord, I receive Your love and forgiveness.

Lord, I believe You. I am overwhelmed with joy because of You. Lord, forgive me for not loving myself as You love me. Entwine my heart with Yours that I may receive Your love, mercy, and forgiveness for myself. Through Jesus's gift of mercy, amen.

GOD LOVES ME.

DAY 17

Spiritual Warfare: Taking Our Position

He raised us up with Christ the exalted One, and we ascended with him into the glorious perfection and authority of the heavenly realm, for we are now co-seated as one with Christ!
—EPHESIANS 2:6 (TPT)

The movie *Battleship* caught my attention when it quoted *The Art of War* by Sun Tzu: "Fight the enemy where they aren't." As I meditated on this, the Lord revealed His battle plan for us. We have been raised with Christ and seated in authority in the heavenly realm, where the enemy cannot go. He cannot enter God's throne room, where we're with Christ, who is at the Father's right hand (Romans 8:34). So often, we war against earthly people. However, scripture tells us that our battle is not against flesh and blood (Ephesians 6:12).

Also consider physical position or posture. In Ephesians 2:6, we are seated, and in 6:10–20, we are to stand. We're to sit and stand, not to pace with worry and doubt. Until the total redemption of Christ, we, as citizens of heaven, live in a fallen and broken world. Things may not look victorious, but by taking a seat in the authority of Christ, we bring the victory of heaven into our circumstances.

The enemy comes against me with lies even now. I'm recovering from a stroke, and while I've experienced amazing miracles, I'm not fully recovered. Satan bombards me with negative thoughts. When I dwell on his negative suggestions, I either stop praying or pray very ineffectively. However, when I take my seat with Christ, God's Spirit within me connects with heaven's victory. And that is hope. The Lord works through my weakness to bring healing to others.

REFLECT

- What battles are you currently waging?
- How can you change your battle plan and position?

Pray

I am a child of God, and I am seated with Christ at His right hand. Satan, you were rendered powerless by Christ's death and resurrection. You must go and can no longer harass _____ with lies and slander.

I'M SEATED WITH CHRIST.

DAY 18

Centering: Expectant Waiting

Yet I believe with all my heart that I will see again your goodness, Yahweh, in the land of life eternal! Here's what I've learned through it all: Don't give up; don't be impatient; be entwined as one with the Lord. Be brave and courageous, and never lose hope. Yes, keep on waiting—for he will never disappoint you!
—PSALM 27:13–14 (TPT)

"Centering." "Silence." "Waiting." These words do not seem to fit in our culture of noise, crowds, and microwaves. Throughout scripture, we are called to wait. We center ourselves in silence to hear the voice of God, to express faith in God, and to seek God's will. Silently waiting before the Lord may feel like we are doing nothing when the exact opposite is true. My dog, while in the obedience ring, provides a beautiful example of active waiting. Although my dog may be sitting or lying down, she is expectantly listening and watching for my next word or signal.

Centering prayer is a simple method of setting up ideal conditions to rest in the quiet awareness of God's presence. The idea is to clear our minds of the clutter and distractions of the world and focus on God. The breath prayers that we have been practicing each day are a form of centering prayer. They briefly take us out of the busyness of life and refocus us on the Lord.

REFLECT

- When was the last time you experienced silence for more than an hour?
- What holds you back from being awake in silence?

Pray

For today's prayer experience, set aside at least 15 minutes. Be ready for distractions to come at you. Have a blank piece of paper and a pen available. When a thought or a task comes to your mind, jot it down so that you can release it until later. During this time, you may hear God's voice; you may feel God's presence; or, hearing and feeling nothing, you may struggle with the activity. Centering prayer is an activity that needs to be practiced and learned. If you struggle with it the first time, try again. Select a comfortable chair and sit in a comfortable position. Then, using the psalm for today, center yourself with the words "eyes to see God's goodness."

SEE GOD'S GOODNESS.

DAY 19

Adoration: Jesus Incarnate

A child has been born for us; a son has been given to us. The responsibility of complete dominion will rest on his shoulders, and his name will be: The Wonderful One! The Extraordinary Strategist! The Mighty God! The Father of Eternity! The Prince of Peace!
—ISAIAH 9:6 (TPT)

What an incredible mystery we who are Christians have on our hands! We worship the Triune God. A God that is three persons, God the Father, God the Son, and God the Holy Spirit. The second person of the Trinity, Jesus, is the Word of Life, God in human form. We are told in scripture that He is worthy to receive glory and praise (Revelation 5:12). The writer of the letter to Hebrews declares His wonder: "The Son is the dazzling radiance of God's splendor, the exact expression of God's true nature—his mirror image! He holds the universe together and expands it by the mighty power of his spoken word. He accomplished for us the complete cleansing of sins, and then took his seat on the highest throne at the right hand of the majestic One" (Hebrews 1:3).

Incarnate is God in the flesh. Because Jesus stepped down from the splendor of heaven and put on flesh, He experienced life on earth as we do. He walked this earth knowing hardship, betrayal, work, and the temptations of the evil one. He began His visible ministry, and then without sin, He died on the cross for all humanity.

REFLECT

- How much time or thought do you give to worshipping the second person of the Trinity?
- Have you made Jesus Lord of your life?

Pray

Lord Yahweh, You are the dazzling radiance of God's splendor. Mighty God are You. Lord Yahweh, You are holy and worthy of praise. Worthy, worthy are You, Lord. I bow before You, Lord Yahweh! Mighty and marvelous are Your miracles, Lord Yahweh, God Almighty! Righteous and true are Your ways, O Sovereign King of the ages! Lord Yahweh, Your love never ends, to You be all the glory.

JESUS, PRINCE OF PEACE.

DAY 20

Dedication: Our Daily Bread

> *This generous God who supplies abundant seed for the farmer, which becomes bread for our meals, is even more extravagant toward you. First he supplies every need, plus more. Then he multiplies the seed as you sow it, so that the harvest of your generosity will grow.*
> —2 CORINTHIANS 9:10 (TPT)

God gives us seed to provide for our needs. And God gives us more than we need, desiring that we would sow these extra resources in and for others.

Prayers dedicating our resources help us release control of our money, things, time, and talents to God. How do we balance this seemingly endless tug-of-war between being filled and filling others? Walking with God is both being *in* His presence and *being* His presence for others. Christ exemplified this by getting up early to be alone with the Father, then pouring out to the crowds. Christ isolated himself in the Father's presence so He could be the Father's presence to others. No matter our physical work, I believe this is our daily calling: purposefully getting into Our Father's presence to receive our daily bread and to receive seed for sowing into others.

This same principle extends to all that God gives us. Once I consume His gifts of money, things, time, and talent, they are no longer available for me to share and sow into others. Our purpose on this earth is to be the light of the kingdom of God. To fulfill our mission, we need to ask for His wisdom about what to do with the resources that He has given us.

REFLECT

- How do you receive your daily bread?
- By consuming all the resources that God has given you, are you eating someone else's bread?

Pray

Father, it is You who supplies all my needs. You know what I need before I can even ask. Of all that You give me, Father, show me what bread is for me is and what is seed meant for others. Amen.

FATHER, SUPPLIER OF MY NEEDS.

DAY 21

Supplication: The Lost Sheep

And you will open their eyes to their true condition, so that they may turn from darkness to the Light and from the power of Satan to the power of God. By placing their faith in me they will receive the total forgiveness of sins and be made holy, taking hold of the inheritance that I give to my children!'
—ACTS 26:18 (TPT)

Spreading the good news of Jesus's salvation is our mission in Christ. In Acts, Jesus gives this mission directive to Paul (26:18) and the Apostles before He ascends into heaven (Matthew 28:19). Jesus declares saving the lost is His assignment (Luke 19:10). He emphasizes its importance through the parable of the lost sheep (Matthew 18:12–14) and the lost coin (Luke 15:8–10). As believers, we should share God's heart for redeeming the lost. Too often, believers are quiet regarding spreading the good news of the Gospel of Jesus Christ. But it is our assignment to share the kingdom Gospel (1 John 3:16).

This is what some refer to as the "second half" of the Gospel, with the first half being our salvation.

One powerful way we partner with God's kingdom is by praying. Praying that God forgives, redeems, and opens eyes is far more powerful than trying to convince someone with arguments and social media posts. Until God opens their eyes to see the light and recognize the darkness they live in, all our persuasive words fall on deaf ears.

REFLECT

If you have accepted the redeeming love of Christ and believe in Him, why are you still here?

Pray

Holy Father, Your love for _____ is so great that You sent Your son Jesus to earth to save _____. I ask that you would open _____'s eyes to see Jesus, that You would open _____'s ears to hear His voice, and that You would soften _____'s heart to receive Your love. Through the amazing love of Jesus Christ may _____ move out of the kingdom of darkness and into the kingdom of Your light. Through the power of the redeeming work of Christ Jesus, amen.

JESUS, OPEN _____'S EYES.

DAY 22

Contrition: Forgiving God

Though the fig tree does not bud and there are no grapes on the vines, though the olive crop fails and the fields produce no food, though there are no sheep in the pen and no cattle in the stalls, yet I will rejoice in the Lord, I will be joyful in God my Savior.
—HABAKKUK 3:17–18 (NIV)

It is Biblical to bring our accusations and anger to God, like Job, David (Psalm 59), and Asaph (Psalm 73). But what about pardoning God? While Job blamed God for his suffering, rather than forgiving God, Job repents when confronted by the glory of His presence. Likewise, David and Asaph move from accusation into declaring the promises and glory of God.

It is my understanding that forgiveness is for the wounded party. It allows the grace and mercy of Christ to flow through the hurt, wash away the bitterness, and precipitate healing. Christ forgave while He was on the cross; Stephen forgave while being stoned.

Confronted with suffering and injustice, our human hearts may blame God. Scripture gives us the model of taking our hurts and accusations to Him. If God shows up before us with the total weight of His glory, as He did with Job, our only response will be to fall on our knees before Him. But it is equally powerful for the Comforter, the Holy Spirit, to guide us into pouring out our grievances in God's presence.

REFLECT

Have you built any barriers that hinder your relationship with God?

Pray

Today's prayer is based on our verse from Habakkuk. Fill in the blanks with items or areas that cause you to struggle in your relationship with God.

God, _____ happened, _____ occurred, and _____ didn't happen. God, I don't understand why You allowed _____, but I forgive. God, I don't understand why _____ happened or is occurring, but I trust. God, although _____, yet I will rejoice in You, I will be joyful in God my Savior.

MERCY FLOWS THROUGH ME.

DAY 23

Spiritual Warfare: Claiming Our Identity

For it was always in his perfect plan to adopt us as his delightful children, through our union with Jesus, the Anointed One, so that his tremendous love that cascades over us would glorify his grace—for the same love he has for the Beloved, Jesus, he has for us. And this unfolding plan brings him great pleasure!
—EPHESIANS 1:5–6 (TPT)

Our identity in Christ has been paid for and is ready for us to claim, then declare it. Declaring God's promises for us aloud engraves His truth in our minds and hearts, and it shows the enemy that we know this truth.

One of the fiercest areas of battle with the evil one is in our own identity. Satan continually feeds us lies designed to convince us we're not who God says we are. But believing and trusting in our position, authority, and inheritance as fully adopted members of the household of God strengthens us against the enemy's attacks.

I was a teen when I first encountered my true identity in Christ as described in Ephesians 1. The words "chosen," "holy," "blameless," "loved," "adopted," "joint heir through Christ," "redeemed," "forgiven," and "God's possession" stood in stark contrast to the messages I received through the media. I struggled to believe all these words applied to me. So, in this crossroads moment, I decided to start small and answer the question "What can I believe today?"

REFLECT

What words do you repeat to yourself about your identity?

Pray

Through Jesus Christ, I am a blessed, chosen, holy, blameless, loved, adopted, redeemed, forgiven, and lavished-on child of the Most High God, marked with the Holy Spirit's seal. And He blessed, chose, loved, adopted, redeemed, forgave, lavished on, and marked me in all His wisdom and understanding with the fullness of His good pleasure. I'm in agreement with all of heaven and stand on Jesus's yes and amen.

I'M A CHILD OF GOD.

DAY 24

Standing: His Promises

So now wrap your heart tightly around the hope that lives within us, knowing that God always keeps his promises!
—HEBREWS 10:23 (TPT)

During a challenging time in my life, I called a friend and told her I could not pray anymore. In response, she told me to stand on the prayers and promises I already had. After this phone call, the Lord led me to the book of Habakkuk and revealed to me this prayer assignment of standing watch (Habakkuk 2:1). My circumstances did not change, but my posture changed. I gave the battle to the Lord, I stood on His promise and watched His victory, and God transformed my position to stand in the high place of triumph.

For today's experience, literally stand on God's "yes" and "amen." You may use your Bible; however, I recommend writing or typing out a specific verse or recent promise you have received. Then, literally stand on it in a strong posture.

REFLECT

- After you pray, how long before you worry or become anxious?
- What is the difference between knock and keep knocking (Luke 11:9) and worry?

Pray

Heavenly Father, fill me with Your peace. Transform my thoughts to think on what is beautiful, what is lovely. Lift my eyes to look to You, and give me the strength to stand on Your word. Close my mouth from uttering words of fear, worry, and rumor. Holy Father, I humbly come before You and ask You to show me Your good works and Your mercy. I face storms, yet I will praise You and give You glory and honor. By and through the holy name of Jesus. Amen.

Lord, Jesus, today I stand on Your "yes" and "amen."

I'M STANDING.

DAY 25

Adoration: His Glory

Yahweh, our Sovereign God, your glory streams from the heavens above, filling the earth with the majesty of your name! People everywhere see your splendor.
—PSALM 8:1 (TPT)

The Oxford English Dictionary defines majesty in two ways. The first definition is "impressive stateliness, dignity, or beauty." And the second is "royal power" or "sovereignty." Both meanings of the word are reflected upon in Psalm 8:1. God is sovereign with authority, power, and dominion, and He is grand with magnificence, splendor, and beauty. His nature, glory, and brilliance are on display through creation (Psalm 19:1). And His wonder lies plainly before all our eyes (Romans 1:20). Sometimes those things that are in plain sight are the hardest to see. And if we take into account the times my children cannot find something, this occurs more often than sometimes.

When we take our eyes off Christ and focus on our earthly circumstances, doubt can creep into our souls. We need the availability of God's glory and majesty so that our hearts can always praise Him.

REFLECT

- How is the glory of God visible on the earth?
- Do you see His glory in your daily life?
- What changes do you need to make to daily see the glory of God?

Pray

Holy Father in heaven, all praise to You. Open my eyes to see Your glory, and open my mouth to tell of Your majesty. You are holy! You are God Almighty! You Are! You are all-powerful. You are glorious. You are light. You are worthy of all praise. You are enthroned in the heavens, and they declare Your glory. You are good and trustworthy. You are my refuge and my shelter. You reign over all. You are justice, goodness, and mercy. You are healer and provider. Your name is above all names. Holy are You!

EYES TO SEE HIS GLORY.

DAY
26

Dedication: Our Children

Let all the little children come to me and never hinder them! Don't you know that God's kingdom exists for such as these?
—MARK 10:14B (TPT)

There are many services and customs of dedicating children to God. Scripture contains stories throughout both the Old and New Testaments of dedicating children to God. Hannah, who was barren until the birth of Samuel, physically gave him to the temple for the work of the Lord. Mary and Joseph took Jesus to the temple to be dedicated. And Jesus told the disciples to allow the children to receive His prayer and blessing.

Prayers of dedication bless children and remind parents to exemplify Christ's love. This reminder is really for all adults. We are to be the light of God's kingdom here on earth, as children are closely watching us.

It is never too early to commit children to the Lord. Likewise, it is never too late. They can be dedicated at any age. Furthermore, it can't be done too often, especially since it calls us to put our lives in order. Instead of praying complaints about our children's mistakes or delinquent ways, let's ask the Lord's blessing over them. Additionally, ask for God's mercy and love to flow through you to them, and ask for the wisdom to live as the light of Christ.

REFLECT

- Are there children (infants to teens) in your life that you influence?
- Are you a living example of Christ for the children in your life?

Pray

Heavenly Father, help me be a living example of Your love, light, mercy, and peace for _____.
May _____ see You through me and my life.
Father, may _____ desire to dedicate their life to You. And I ask that You bless _____ and keep _____; that You will make Your face shine on _____ and be gracious to _____; that You turn your face toward _____ and give _____ peace. Through the love of Jesus, amen.

CHILDREN ARE GOD'S BLESSING.

DAY 27

Supplication: Comfort for Grief

How content you become when you weep with complete brokenness, for you will laugh with unrestrained joy.
—LUKE 6:21B (TPT)

Life is uncertain, and it is impossible to be prepared for the horrible occasions of sickness, suffering, distress, or death. In the face of the prosperity gospel is Jesus's unwanted promise of John 16:33: "In this unbelieving world you will experience trouble and sorrows." Yet, where there is misfortune, it is critical to consistently recall that there is another existence with God both now and in eternity. However, regardless of the amount of comfort we attempt to receive from this knowledge, we grieve.

When the crushing weight of grief crashes down and takes my very breath away, when illness strikes and grabs hold, when a panic attack suddenly sets in, when I have put myself in time-out because I have miserably failed and the weight of God's mercy is more than I feel I can stand, when cruel words fill my ears, when my dreams seem to have failed, when all around seems shattered and lost, that is the moment that Jesus sees my heart, and He weeps. He holds me, and He weeps. And in the moment of my grief, that is enough.

REFLECT

- How do the words "Jesus wept" make you feel?
- Do you believe that the promise "Jesus heals the brokenhearted" is for you?

Pray

For self: Jesus sees, knows, and loves. He experienced this pain for me, and He experiences this pain with me now. Jesus wept for me, and He weeps with me. Jesus has not forsaken me. He comforts me under the shelter of His wing. I lean into You, Jesus. Hold me, and don't let go.

For others: Jesus sees, knows, and loves _____. He experienced this pain for _____, and He experiences this pain with _____ now. Jesus wept for _____, and He weeps with _____. Jesus has not forsaken _____. He comforts _____ under the shelter of His wing. _____, lean into Jesus. Jesus, hold _____, and may they feel Your arms of love.

JESUS SEES ME.

DAY 28

Contrition: Releasing Resentment

Because you begged me, I forgave you the massive debt that you owed me. Why didn't you show the same mercy to your fellow servant that I showed to you?
—MATTHEW 18:32–33 (TPT)

When we hold on to criticism, condemnation, and resentment, either after saying we have forgiven someone or as a roadblock to forgiveness, our eyes, hearts, and minds stay focused on the person. This takes our eyes off God. Within scripture, there is the principle of becoming like what we behold. I like to refer to this as focus-directed transformation. According to 2 Corinthians 3:18, we become transformed into His likeness as we look on the Lord's glory. Likewise, if we concentrate with comparison or contempt on someone, we begin to conform to their ways (2 Corinthians 10:12). And Psalm 115 goes so far as to say if we continue to look at dead idols, we will become dead like them. We destroy ourselves when we continue to walk in bitterness because when we focus on what we do not like in someone, we become conformed to that characteristic in our own lives.

Releasing judgments and woundedness against someone or a group of people does not mean we are saying what they did was right or okay. God offers mercy and forgiveness to us without saying likewise. Additionally, it is not justification or recommendation for someone to stay in a dangerous or harmful situation. However, it is saying that we will allow God's forgiveness to flow through us. We are going to refocus our eyes on Jesus and receive the healing of the Holy Spirit. And we are no longer going to stand before God's throne as an accuser.

REFLECT

- Do you spend time dwelling on how someone wronged you?
- Are you able to truly pray for your enemy?

Pray

Holy Father, forgive me. I have criticized, condemned, and resented _____. I have not allowed Your love and mercy to flow through me. Father, I hold no accusation against _____ and release them into the hands of Jesus.

LORD, GRANT _____ MERCY.

DAY 29

Spiritual Warfare: Prophetic Intercession

At times we don't even know how to pray, or know the best things to ask for.
—ROMANS 8:26 (TPT)

Prophetic intercessors pray God's will and heart into the things of earth. In the ninth chapter of his book *Praying with God's Heart*, James W. Goll describes prophetic intercession in the following three ways: It is the ability to receive an immediate prayer request from God, it is waiting to hear and receive God's burden, and, lastly, it is praying with God.

Often, prophetic intercession is easier to learn and practice when praying for people we do not know very well. For a time, my church placed prayer boxes in stores, beauty salons, doctor's offices, and other locations. We collected the requests each week and prayed over them. I received powerful testimonies from the intercessors. Since they didn't know the details of the requests or the requestor, they had to wait on the Holy Spirit to tell them how to pray.

Prophetic intercession is releasing control of our desired outcome and joining with the Holy Spirit to pray and intercede for His desired outcome.

REFLECT

- How do you pray for people and situations?
- When you pray, do you ask God for His plans and purposes?

Pray

Be willing to release control of your plans and agenda. Allow the Holy Spirit to highlight what He wants you to pray about, then listen for how He wants you to pray. And pray along with the heart of God. Additional practice: Ask the Holy Spirit to highlight people He wants you to pray over throughout your day. As you encounter them, ask the Holy Spirit how He wants you to pray. In a trusted group gathering, have prayer requests submitted by name only. Then ask the Holy Spirit how He is praying and pray along with Him.

Holy Spirit, I give You my eyes, my ears, and my heart. Open them that I may hear and know how You are interceding. Align my words and my prayers with Your prayers. In Jesus's name, amen.

OPEN MY EARS TO HEAR.

DAY 30

Resting: Abiding

So you must remain in life-union with me, for I remain in life-union with you.
—JOHN 15:4 (TPT)

In the creation account from Genesis 1, God says let the waters teem with fish, the air be filled with birds, and the land produce living creatures, all according to their kind. However, when He creates mankind, it's not according to our kind but in His image. Notice that the fish, birds, and living creatures are to occupy water, sky, and ground. But then God fills humans with His very breath of life. We were created in His image, with His life-breath, and to abide in Him. Jesus's death and resurrection restore us into this life-union with God. The prayer of Jesus for us in John 17 speaks to this abiding when He prays that we would be one with Him.

This scripture points to God abiding in and through us, but how do we abide in Christ? J. C. Ryle explains, "To abide in Christ means to keep up a habit of constant close communion with Him—to be always leaning on Him, resting on Him, pouring out our hearts to Him, and using Him as our Fountain of life." This is God's original plan for us in creation that we would abide in Him, and He would be our source and purpose for living. I believe the opposite of abiding in Christ is defined by the warning to not devote the affections of our hearts to the ways of this world (1 John 2:15). Whatever becomes the focus of the desires of our heart becomes the fountain of our life. And this is what pours out of us for others to see.

REFLECT

How do you keep in close communion with God? How do you rest on Him?

Pray

Jesus tells His disciples to live in Him in John 15:1–11. Slowly read these words and underline any word or phrase that resonates deeply within you. Repeat these words or phrases.

Use one of the phrases or the suggested breath prayer to practice communion with God's presence throughout the day. Set a planned time interval such as every hour or every half hour to breathe in the presence of God. Take a deep breath, then exhale your breath prayer.

ME IN GOD AND GOD IN ME.

DAY 31

Adoration: Stronghold and Refuge

God, you're such a safe and powerful place to find refuge! You're a proven help in time of trouble—more than enough and always available whenever I need you.
—PSALM 46:1 (TPT)

During times of difficulty, not praising God is a symptom that doubt is creeping into our hearts. As we go through the conflicts and crises of our days, we need a powerful and available refuge. Nahum 1:7, Psalm 9:9, and Psalm 46:1 are just a few of the many proclamations of God's sanctuary by the Old Testament writers. And in Acts 1, Jesus tells the disciples that they will be filled with power at the arrival of the Holy Spirit. Thus, God's safety and protection for us is both prevailing and obtainable.

When I first began attending church after my stroke, I was in a wheelchair, and standing was difficult. I couldn't close my eyes because my sense of balance was off. Often not even opening my mouth, I would just sit during the time of worship. Songs of praise began tugging at my heart during this period. In order to stand against our spiritual enemy, who can often take us out within our own thoughts, we have to speak the words of praise and proclaim God's protection within our circumstances and trials.

REFLECT

What in your current circumstances makes it hard to praise the Lord?

Pray

Proclaim God as your stronghold and protector. The praise below is based on Psalm 46.

Holy Father, You are my refuge. You are my strength! I praise Your name. You are my help. You are with me in the middle of _____ (name your current struggle). You are my tower of strength, and I trust You. Although the earth gives way and the mountains fall into the heart of the sea, and _____ (name your current struggle) occurs, I will not fear. I will dwell in the shelter of Your wings. You are my fortress and my protection. You are God.

THE LORD IS MY STRENGTH.

DAY 32

Dedication: Hope for the Future

For I know the plans I have for you, declares the Lord, plans to prosper you and not to harm you, plans to give you hope and a future.
—JEREMIAH 29:11 (NIV)

We tend to worry about so many things. We worry about what we will do, about who we should be, and about our needs. God's word tells us that He'll not only take care of our needs for today, but He also has a plan for our future. Prayers of dedicating our future help us surrender our control over what will be.

For me, surrendering my future and walking in the calling of His footsteps is not a one-and-done type of prayer. I find I must continually allow the Holy Spirit to move me back into the hands of the Potter. It is easy for me to make plans and then ask God to bless them. However, the Lord calls us to join Him in His plans.

Additionally, there is no room for both worry and hope within our spirits. "Your will be done" should not be throwing up our hands in exasperation, giving in, and then doing nothing. It is actively surrendering our will and control over to God's desire and plans. It is trusting that God created us and designed us. It is believing that He wants and needs our gifts and talents.

REFLECT

- Do you make plans first and then hope that God will bless them?
- How do you stop and seek God's will for your future?

Pray

Dedicating your future to the Lord is a prayer of trust. It is releasing worry and allowing the Holy Spirit to replace your anxious thoughts with hope. The prayer below is based on Romans 15:13 and Jeremiah 29:11.

Abba, Holy Father, You are my fountain of hope. I release to You all control of my future and trust in the plan You have for me. Father, I give You tomorrow, and I give You _____ (plans and dreams). Lord, I ask that You replace my worry and fear about tomorrow with Your uncontainable joy and perfect peace. And may the power of the Holy Spirit continually surround my life with Your superabundance until I radiate with hope! Through the work of Jesus, amen.

THY WILL.

DAY 33

Supplication: His Voice

My own sheep will hear my voice and I know each one, and they will follow me.
—JOHN 10:27 (TPT)

God's voice and word are what Isaiah calls real bread (Isaiah 55). For prayer to be the conduit for our relationship, we need to learn to hear God. Many believers say that they do not hear God's voice. Since He calls us to a life of never-ending prayer, I firmly believe He continually speaks to us. We must learn how to hear Him. Don't be discouraged. Even Samuel, a prophet of Israel, didn't recognize God's voice the first time he heard it.

God speaks through His word, His creation, and His Spirit within us. One of the best ways to hear Him is to consistently be in His word. Knowing how Christ speaks also helps us to hear Him (John 10:27).

He may speak through a vision or dream, or through nature. And He speaks through His Spirit within us. We are all different and will hear His Spirit in our unique way.

Some ways of hearing God include a deep sense of knowing, a thought, a verse or reference coming to mind, a vision, or a physical sensation. In Psalm 32, God says that He will instruct and teach us. We should be willing students and let go of the lie that God doesn't speak. This is the job of the Holy Spirit dwelling within us. He speaks and tells us of the things of God, He comforts us, and He points us to Christ. Jeremiah 33:3 says God will show us things we don't know. He longs to tell us more than we can think or imagine.

REFLECT

- Do you believe God is speaking to you?
- When things that you are praying about line up, do you call it God or a coincidence?

Pray

Holy Father, thank You for giving me Your Spirit. Father, forgive me for listening to the voices of this world. I want to hear Your voice. You promise that Your sheep will hear and know Your voice. Jesus, I declare that You are my Lord and Savior, and I am one of your sheep. Open my ears to hear Your voice. Give me the wisdom to know it is You speaking to my heart through my inner being. Speak, Lord, I am listening.

LORD, SPEAK; I'M LISTENING.

DAY
34

Contrition: Surrender

God, I invite your searching gaze into my heart.
—PSALM 139:23 (TPT)

As we have prayed through the forgiveness petition of the Lord's Prayer, we have asked for salvation, affirmed our faith, offered forgiveness, and released bitterness. Today, we are going deeper in our repentance. The Holy Spirit is most often gentle in His nudges of correction. He waits for our response, and then He presses deeper. This process brings us into the image of Christ. We are not pursuing the answer to the popular question "What would Jesus do?" but instead, as Dallas Willard says, "What would Jesus do if He was you?"

Psalm 139 brings us to the "God only knows" encounter. Through the words, the Holy Spirit lovingly deepens and restores our intimacy and identity. He calls us to a position of love that causes us to choose humility. And He gives us the grace to practice forgiveness and repentance in our daily life. When our motivation is love, we have the ability to maintain this lifestyle. Praying Psalm 139 is not about learning another formula, but about embracing a process of encounter from a posture of humility. This posture engages the Lord's heart and compels Him to draw near. In Psalm 139, we learn David's strategy for pursuing God's heart.

REFLECT

- Are you afraid of something the Holy Spirit may reveal?
- Is there something in your past you are trying to hide?

Pray

Lord, You know everything about me. And You love me. You formed my innermost being, shaping me both inside and out in my mother's womb. You _____ (spend time praising God for what He has done in your life). Holy Spirit, I invite You to gaze into my heart, examine me, find out everything that may be hidden within, sift through all my anxious thoughts. Make sure I'm walking on the right path, and lead me in Your glorious and everlasting way. Amen.

SEARCH ME AND KNOW ME.

DAY 35

Spiritual Warfare: Overcoming Shame

The Lord Yahweh empowers me, so I am not humiliated. For that reason, with holy determination, I will do his will and not be ashamed.
—ISAIAH 50:7 (TPT)

Shame is a fierce battleground. The evil one attacks us with shame over our past, challenging our belief in our freedom from condemnation (Romans 8:1). Most often, these attacks come as an internal conversation. A negative thought enters our mind, and instead of taking it captive (2 Corinthians 10:5), we allow it to fester in our hearts. By doing so we enable the enemy to turn "I did something bad, and I'm forgiven" into "I am bad and unforgivable." The only way to win this battle is to stand on the truth of God's word: that we are chosen, called from darkness into light, and part of His royal priesthood (1 Peter 2:9). He lavished His love on us and calls us children of God (1 John 3:1). And He chose us before the creation of the world (Ephesians 1:4–5). When we repent, He forgives and removes our transgressions from us as far as the East is from the West (Psalm 103).

The second battle of shame comes as a fear to do His will. We are afraid of what others will think. We become paralyzed to pray bold prayers out of fear that He might not answer. Or we are ashamed to do His will because we are afraid of what He might ask us to do. Remember: God's promise is that when we seek Him first and when we passionately pursue Him, He will provide (Matthew 6:33, Psalm 34:10).

REFLECT

- Are you holding on to past failures?
- Has the Holy Spirit prompted you to do something you chose not to do because of what others might have thought?

Pray

Yahweh, I believe Your promise that although my sins stained me like scarlet, You have whitened them like bright, new-fallen snow! I am delivered from fear and shame. Lord, I want to have a willing heart. Give me strength and desire to obey You that I may feast on Your blessings. Amen.

I AM OF THE ROYAL PRIESTHOOD.

DAY 36

Thanksgiving: Be of Good Cheer

For in this unbelieving world you will experience trouble and sorrows, but you must be courageous, [cheer up] for I have conquered the world!
—JOHN 16:33 (TPT)

We give thanks to God in everything, not because the situation is good but because God is. On a recent vacation, I found myself sitting on a bench while my family explored the trails of the mountain summit. I waited, inwardly complaining that I was physically unable to hike. A lady, also unable to climb, came and shared my bench. As we spoke, the Lord opened my heart to His love for her. I prayed for her, and God lifted my eyes to His love through the beauty around me. I still sat, but my heart rejoiced.

Once, God also showed me what conquering the world means to Him. During one of my friend's last nights fighting cancer, I knelt praying in her bedroom. In anger, I beat my fists, asking God to heal her. I had fasted, wept, and prayed! As I cried out, He gently said, "I have prepared a place for her at My table." "No!" my soul screamed. "Her spilt blood is unjust." He said, "The very ground cries at the blood spilled unjustly. This is the sound that always fills My ears. Can you stand it?" And I heard the horrible noise of rocks groaning, crying under strain. I couldn't bear it. "The ground cries out for My justice, but My mercy is here." And I saw Jesus on His throne, weeping with the saints, as a river flowed of His healing.

Jesus has overcome. He stepped down from His throne to bear our sin and suffering. He ignores creation's plea to make it end and weeps with me. And that is enough for me to choose His unspeakable joy.

REFLECT

- Are there things in your life preventing you from being of good cheer?
- How can the joy of the Lord become your strength daily?

Pray

Lord, do not let my heart be offended by all the trouble and trials around me. Instill me with the ready purpose of looking toward heaven and fill me with the joy of Your Spirit that I will be strengthened and renewed. Through the power of Jesus's name, amen.

EYES ON GOD.

DAY

37

Adoration: Living Word

In the beginning the Living Expression was already there. And the Living Expression was with God, yet fully God.
—JOHN 1:1 (TPT)

In Psalm 119, David declares his undying love for God's word. At the time of the writing of this psalm, the only written word of God available to him was the first five books of the Old Testament. And still, David unashamedly proclaims that it is his song, hope, comfort; it is beautiful; and it gives him life. Through the beautiful language of the opening chapter of John, we can make the connection to Jesus. He is the Living Word. In the Passion Translation, the Greek term *Logos* is translated as the "Living Expression." Many versions render this term as "Word." However, it is wrong to think of the use here as merely an element of a sentence. Instead, Logos is a form of self-disclosure or eternal message. The Christ, the Living Word, is the living expression of the visible God.

In his letter to the Ephesians, Paul tells us that our only spiritual offensive weapon is the sword of the spirit, which is the word of God. This is Jesus. It is through Jesus that we hear, see, and experience the fulfillment of God's promises. Jesus, slain for us, is worthy of all praise.

REFLECT

- Do you spend time praising Jesus?
- How do you express your love and adoration to Christ?

Pray

Making the connection between David's word of God in Psalm 119 and John's Word, today's prayer of praise is based on Psalm 119. To press deeper into the characteristics of the Word, read Psalm 119 and underline all the acclaims of God's word, then write out your own prayer of praise or use the one provided.

Yahweh, Living Word, You are worthy of all praise. You are light and life. You give strength, and You are faithful and true. You are the greatest treasure. You are my delight and full of miraculous wonders. You, Lord, are holy and full of splendor. Grace upon grace, You freely pour out. Your tender love overwhelms me. You rescue, redeem, and restore. You are my hope and confidence. You, Yahweh, are worthy of all praise!

JESUS, MY LIVING HOPE.

DAY 38

Dedication: My Inner Being

I heard your voice in my heart say, "Come, seek my face;" my inner being responded, "Yahweh, I'm seeking your face with all my heart."
—PSALM 27:8 (TPT)

Sometimes it's easy to feel like aspects of our culture operate on the materialistic level of seeking things, outward perfection, and influence. Regardless of our earthly circumstances, as believers in the Son of God, we are called not to imitate the things of this world (Romans 12:2). And by devoting our inner being to seeking Christ, we will continually be renewed even though our physical bodies are decaying (2 Corinthians 4:16–18).

The Lord's invitation is not dependent on our current condition. We don't have to clean ourselves up first. He calls us to come as we are and respond to His invitation. Paul says that once He encountered Christ, he gave up all his past accomplishments to be enriched in the fullness of knowing Christ Jesus (Philippians 3:7).

We place our hearts and minds in the position of receiving inner transformation by dedicating our inner being to seeking the Lord. Using the prayer from Ephesians 3:16–17, we ask God to strengthen us and to root our lives in Christ.

REFLECT

- Do you spend more time on earthly pursuit than inward transformation?
- What steps can you take to allow inward transformation by the Holy Spirit?

Pray

Since our actions begin with our thoughts (James 1:14), an overhaul of our thoughts away from our culture allows for Holy Spirit transformation (Romans 12:2). Today's prayer of dedicating our inner being focuses on surrendering our thought life to the Holy Spirit.

Holy Spirit, I surrender my inner being to the work of Your transformation. Strengthen my heart, mind, and will to think on what is honorable, beautiful, respectful, pure, holy, merciful, and kind. Holy Spirit, when my thoughts wander, redirect them to the glorious work of God. In the holy name of Jesus, amen.

HOLY SPIRIT, YOUR THOUGHTS.

DAY 39

Supplication: Manifestations of the Spirit

Each believer is given continuous revelation by the Holy Spirit to benefit not just himself but all.
—1 CORINTHIANS 12:7 (TPT)

Jesus said when the Holy Spirit comes, we have power. This power isn't just to benefit the individual, but all. Jesus connected this power with witnessing for Him (Acts 1:8). This outward evidence of the Holy Spirit is required of witnesses for God. Scripture reveals God's actions on earth, from parting the Red Sea through Moses to restoring Paul's eyesight through Ananias to healing people as Peter's shadow passed over them to healing through Paul's handkerchiefs. While the church disagrees about gifts of the Holy Spirit, nothing scriptural negates Jesus's statement that with the coming of the Holy Spirit, we will have power.

God's gifts will confirm His words and expand His kingdom. Some ignore them, some abuse them for personal gain. Still, they are divine power of the body of Christ on earth. The suffering world needs the gifts of heavenly wisdom, encouragement, and divine healing. I've been blessed to be both a recipient of and to manifest these gifts. As a result of my stroke, I experienced a blind spot in my left peripheral vision. Medical professionals told me that eyesight issues would not recover, and in rehab, I was taught to turn my head to compensate for this blind spot. The Lord, however, restored my peripheral vision through the prayers of others.

REFLECT

- Are you afraid of the visible evidence of the Holy Spirit?
- What is your motivation for seeking the visible expressions of the Holy Spirit?

Pray

Today's prayer is based on the encouragement from 1 Corinthians 12:31 that we should seek with passion the gifts of the Spirit.

Sweet Holy Spirit, transform my heart to trust in You entirely. I release all that I am to Your Spirit, that Your overwhelming love and compassion for everyone will be evidenced through me. Available to me because of the work of Christ Jesus, amen.

HOLY SPIRIT REVEALED THROUGH ME.

DAY 40

Contrition: Releasing Pride

God resists you when you are proud but multiplies grace and favor when you are humble.
—JAMES 4:6 (TPT)

God's word calls us to humility and says that He stands against the proud. In living a life of humility, we are given Jesus as our example. Instead of grasping at equality with God, the perfect son of God stepped down from heaven. But how do we release pride and live humbly? As soon as we try to self-examine our condition concerning humility, pride wells up within us. Additionally, in trying to walk in humility, we often fall into false humility, which is pride in disguise. Both pride and false humility are rooted in thinking of ourselves first.

Once as I was struggling to write a devotion, I felt the Lord urging me to reach out and ask for prayer. For a while, I resisted. I wanted to be able to write from my own strength and understanding. And I didn't want others to see me as less spiritual, less knowledgeable, or less capable. However, once I reached out and asked for help, I received the most beautiful, uplifting, and encouraging prayers. This is the picture of the reality of today's verse. As long as I was too prideful before the Lord, He resisted me. However, once I humbled myself and admitted I was struggling, the Lord's grace and mercy, along with the words for today's devotional, flowed.

REFLECT

- Do you struggle to ask God or others for help?
- Do you always have the correct answers?

Pray

The first step in releasing pride is to acknowledge that we need God. This prayer for releasing pride is practically walking out Romans 12:16 in our daily interactions with others.

Dear heavenly Father, forgive me for walking in pride. Forgive me for thinking of myself more than _____. Lord, all that I am, all that I have is because of You and for Your glory. Apart from You, Lord, I can't do anything. Holy Spirit, give me eyes to see others as You have created them and to value their thoughts, their gifts, and their talents. Give me a heart that is both willing to serve and willing to be served. In and for Jesus's name, amen.

LORD, I NEED YOU.

DAY 41

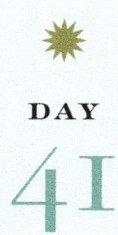

Spiritual Warfare: Overcoming Fear

> *I leave the gift of peace with you—my peace. Not the kind of fragile peace given by the world, but my perfect peace. Don't yield to fear or be troubled in your hearts—instead, be courageous!*
> —JOHN 14:27 (TPT)

When we say goodbye to our loved ones, we often tell them to be careful; however, Jesus's parting words include "be courageous." Much of Jesus's teaching addresses our hearts concerning fear. Jesus tells us not to be anxious about what we will eat or wear (Luke 12:22–24). Additionally, fear does not come from Him (2 Timothy 1:7). He, however, knows we're afraid and continually tells His people to fear not.

    Simply choosing not to be afraid doesn't work. As soon as the decision is made, our whole body can become overwhelmed with more thoughts and feelings of dread. When I recognized anxiousness, worry, and fear as harassing spirits of the evil one, I began to walk in victory over fear. At first, I would claim the words of Luke 10:19, declaring authority to trample fear. It would subside for a time, but to my dismay, it returned. This happened until I saw that Jesus offers peace in place of fear. And the Holy Spirit offers power, love, and self-control. When I asked the Holy Spirit to fill me with these things, there was no room for my heart to be troubled with fear and worry.

REFLECT

- Are you troubled or anxious about tomorrow?
- Do you allow fear for yourself or your loved ones to consume your thoughts?

Pray

By the authority of Christ Jesus within me, spirit of fear, you must go. Spirit of worry and anxiousness, I no longer give you place in my heart and mind, and you must go, in the name of Jesus. Holy Spirit, come and fill me with the fullness of your fruit. Fill me with your peace, power, love, and self-control, and may I be courageous for the name of Jesus. Amen.

I TRUST YOU, LORD.

DAY 42

Lamenting: A Broken Heart

I'm worn out with my weeping and groaning. Night after night I soak my pillow with tears, and flood my bed with weeping.
—PSALM 6:6 (TPT)

Prayers of lament can be for ourselves, others, our church, or our nation. Psalm 6 is a personal song of remorse and repentance. Tears of lament result in redemption and hope, while whines of despair leave us wallowing in guilt and lack. Many Psalms model lament, while instructions for how to lament are found in Joel, Jeremiah, and James.

In deep prayers of lament, we see both the current condition and God's completed plan. And then we join with the Holy Spirit in weeping over the gap between the two. Psalm 126 conveys the picture of being in this gap. We sow in tears while rejoicing over the great miracles He has done before and calling on the Lord to do it again. In a life that is full of pain and sorrow, prayers of lament allow us to bring our hurts before God. Within the Psalms, there are many examples of laments. They cover personal issues, communal grief, and national suffering. We are permitted to approach God in our grief and sorrow and receive the grace that we need to strengthen us in our weakness (Hebrews 4:16).

REFLECT

- Do the things of this life break your heart?
- Do you hope through your lament?

Pray

Use the following prompts to write out your own prayer of lament. Ask the Lord to break your heart for what breaks His. Talk about your pain and sorrow to Him and call on Him to remember His promises. Allow yourself space to weep.

Lord, my heart is broken over _____. How long, oh Lord, will You allow _____? You have done _____ before. I call on You to remember Your promise of _____. Lord, break in and _____ (redeem, restore, rebuild). Lord, I will trust in Your goodness. I hope in Your promise of _____.

LORD, BREAK MY HEART.

DAY 43

Adoration: Our Ascended Lord

Right after Jesus spoke those words, the disciples saw him being lifted into the sky, and disappearing into a cloud!
—ACTS 1:9 (TPT)

The church spends much time and effort celebrating the birth of Jesus as a human. Likewise, we reflect on His death on the cross and His resurrection. How much time do we spend rejoicing over His ascension into heaven? But for the line in the Apostle's Creed, "He ascended into heaven, and sits at the right hand of God the Father almighty," the church calendar skips over His ascension, seemingly jumping from Easter to Pentecost. However, in Jesus's prayer the night before His crucifixion, one of the requests that He makes of God the Father is that we would see Him in His glory (John 17). We see Jesus in His humility, born as a baby lying in a manger. We see Him in His brokenness, dying on a cross. And we see Him raised with Mary in the garden. But can we, as we walk this earth, see Him in His glory? As Stephen was about to be stoned, he proclaimed his vision of seeing heaven opening before him and seeing Jesus at the right of God (Acts 7:54–55). One way for us to envision our ascended Lord is to worship Him as our ascended Lord—to give Him praise in His position at the right hand of the Father.

REFLECT

- Have you spent time reflecting on our ascended Lord?
- When Jesus prayed that we would see Him in His glory, do you believe it is for us now?

Pray

Jesus, worthy of all praise, You are ascended into heaven. You stand at the right hand of the Father Almighty. You are enthroned and exalted. You continue Your work of intercession for me and are the founder and perfecter of my faith. All authority is subject to You, Great High Priest. You are the radiance of God's glory. You hold the seven stars and walk among the seven golden lampstands. The Beginning and the End, Your words pierce hearts, Your eyes are blazing fire, and Your feet are like burnished brass. You hold the sevenfold Spirit of God, True One. You have David's key, open doors that no one can shut, and close doors that no one can open. You are the Amen, the faithful and true witness, and the ruler of God's creation. All praise to You, Ascended Lord.

JESUS AT THE FATHER'S RIGHT HAND.

DAY 44

Dedication: Control

Don't be pulled in different directions or worried about a thing. Be saturated in prayer throughout each day, offering your faith-filled requests before God with overflowing gratitude. Tell him every detail of your life, then God's wonderful peace that transcends human understanding will guard your heart and mind through Jesus Christ.
—PHILIPPIANS 4:6–7 (TPT)

The whole purpose of God taking Jeremiah to the potter's house was to give a visible example of how God lovingly tends our lives when we release complete control to Him. While Jeremiah's vision was for the entire nation of Israel, it is also true for our individual lives. When we are on the Master's wheel, we do not have to be worried about the outcome or the next step, for it is all in God's hands. However, when we take responsibility from within our own strength, we become overwhelmed with worry and doubt.

When the Lord first called me out of full-time employment with NASA, I became anxious about what was next. I didn't wait on the Lord and began filling my time with things I thought were good. This included taking classes, getting certifications, and volunteering. I had jumped off the potter's wheel, and I was wearing busyness as a badge of honor. My life was so full of commitments that I had already made. When the Lord did reveal His next step, I was not in a position to take it. I had to first release the things I had taken hold of to move as He called me.

REFLECT

- Are there areas of your life that you have not released control of to God?
- Instead of trying to fit God time into your life, what would it look like to move your whole life into God?
- Is your impression that following God results in misery and hardship?

Pray

Prayers of dedication mean surrendering the worry and responsibility of creating and living in our kingdoms for the peace and joy of living in God's kingdom.

Holy Father, forgive me for jumping out of Your hands and trying to create and establish myself in the image of me. Lord Jesus, I release control of my life and my plans into Your hands so that Your peace may guard my heart and mind. In Jesus's name, amen.

GOD'S WILL BE DONE.

DAY 45

Supplication: Our Nation and Our World

> *Most of all, I'm writing to encourage you to pray with gratitude to God. Pray for all men with all forms of prayers and requests as you intercede with intense passion. And pray for every political leader and representative, so that we would be able to live tranquil, undisturbed lives, as we worship the awe-inspiring God with pure hearts.*
> —1 TIMOTHY 2:1–2 (TPT)

If the people of God would humble themselves and pray, God promises to heal our land (2 Chronicles 7:12). Additionally, we are told to pray for the peace and prosperity of the country we find ourselves in because if it prospers, we will also prosper. Scripture calls us to pray for our nation and our leaders. This injunction to intercede is not only for the nations and leaders that we like but also for those we do not like.

REFLECT

- Do you pray for your city, state, and nation?
- Do you intercede for the nations of the world?

Pray

Many things can be prayed for the nations and our leaders. I choose to pray from the words of scripture that they would be washed in the healing power of the love of God. Today's prayer is from Ephesians 3:14–21.

On behalf of the nation of _____, I fall to my knees before the Father, from whom all in heaven and on earth derives its name. Father, out of Your glorious riches, please strengthen the people of the nation of _____ with power through Your Spirit in their inner being so that Christ may dwell in their hearts through faith. May the people of _____ be rooted and established in love and be able to understand how wide and long and high and deep is the love of Christ. May they know this love that surpasses knowledge so that they may be filled with all the fullness of God. To You, Father, who is able to do immeasurably more than I ask or imagine, to You be glory in the church and in Christ Jesus throughout all generations, forever and ever! Amen.

FATHER, FORGIVE US.

DAY 46

Contrition: On Behalf of Others

We continually share in the death of Jesus in our own bodies so that the resurrection life of Jesus will be revealed through our humanity.
—2 CORINTHIANS 4:10 (TPT)

Many of us don't want to accept responsibility for our failures, much less for the sin or failures of others. In addition to forgiving those who offend us, we're also called to plead God's forgiveness for others, even before those in need of forgiveness realize it. We witness this within scripture. Christ, with His dying breath, called out to God to "forgive them for they do not know what they do" (Luke 23:34). Stephen asks Jesus not to hold the sin of those stoning him against them. In the Old Testament, Job prayed for God to forgive his children. Samuel prayed for the forgiveness of Israel. Solomon prayed for the forgiveness of his nation.

Moses frequently pleaded with God to forgive a sinful nation, offering to sacrifice himself for them (Exodus 32:31–32). Jeremiah, Daniel, Ezra, and Nehemiah interceded for their nations by identifying with their communal guilt.

One day while watching my son and his high school marching band rehearse, I witnessed this concept unfold. Anytime a mistake was made, the director yelled for someone to take responsibility for it. I watched as time and time again my son and other section leaders stepped forward to spare others within their sections. This is what we do. We can act on behalf of others, drawing suffering upon ourselves, which can release life into our community.

REFLECT

- Have you thought of repenting on behalf of others?
- How do you feel about Moses's plea to be blotted out in place of the Israelites?

Pray

Repenting on behalf of others is the concept of transference of forgiveness. Not only did Jesus say this in words from on the cross, it is in His very act of dying on the cross for us.

Holy Father, per Your great love, forgive _____ for _____. Because of the grace and mercy of Jesus Christ. Amen.

FATHER, FORGIVE THEM.

DAY 47

Spiritual Warfare: Closing Doors

Go, my people, into your inner chambers and close the doors behind you. Hide for a little while, until his indignation is over.
—ISAIAH 26:20 (TPT)

God's example for us in the fiercest battle is for us to withdraw into His sanctuary, close the door, and allow Him to fight. We tend to view this withdrawing as a failed retreat, and instead of hiding in God's shelter, we leave the door wide open and tremble in fear. Jesus calls us to enter into His providence and grace by praying in our inner chambers with a closed door (Matthew 6:6). Other ways we leave the door open include trying to battle the enemy by ourselves out of our own strength or staying by the cracked open door to watch. As believers in Christ, we are called to close all doors to darkness.

The enemy comes to steal, kill, and destroy. When we leave doors open to him, we give him an invitation for an easy attack. Some of the doors we leave open as an invitation to evil include disobedience, anger, unforgiveness, idol worship, and unhealed trauma. The Lord Jesus both releases us from the captivity of darkness and heals us from its lingering effects.

REFLECT

- Reread the list of possible open doors. Do you recognize any in your own life?
- Do you experience triggers that result in crushing emotional responses?

Pray

Jesus came to give us abundant life. Abundant includes freedom from the torment of the power of darkness. Today's prayer may be maintenance in your vigilance against the influence of the evil one in your life, or it may be the beginning, the first step to your healing and wholeness.

Holy Lord Jesus, thank You for Your free gift of grace in my life. Holy Spirit, open my eyes, ears, and heart to any possible openings to the evil one in my life and grant me the wisdom to close them. By the authority of Jesus Christ, I close all doors to darkness, I close the door of _____. Holy Spirit, grant me strength to enter the sanctuary of God and commune with Him. Through the power of Christ Jesus at work within my life, amen.

HIDDEN IN JESUS.

DAY 48

Centering: Voicing Prayers

As the snow and rain that fall from heaven do not return until they have accomplished their purpose, soaking the earth and causing it to sprout with new life, providing seed to sow and bread to eat. So also will be the word that I speak; it does not return to me unfulfilled. My word performs my purpose and fulfills the mission I sent it out to accomplish.
—ISAIAH 55:10–11 (TPT)

Today's centering prayer experience focuses on the power of God's word. This reflection moves off our thoughts, beginning with the power of God's spoken word through the power of God within us and ending with the discovery of the power of our spoken words.

In preparing for centering, find a quiet and comfortable place. It is essential to silence our outside influences in order to press deep inside, allowing our inner being to commune with the Spirit of God within us.

REFLECT

- Do you claim God's promises by saying them out loud?
- Do you feel it is vital to pray out loud?

Pray

This time of reflection will begin with an invitation for God to join you. After the opening prayer, take a slow, deep breath and then release it before softly saying each of the following truths from God's word. After speaking that last truth, remain in the position of listening, using one of the truths to refocus your thoughts as they become distracted.

Holy Father, I am here. Speak; I am listening. Protect my heart and mind from the influence of the evil one. I only want to hear Your voice of truth.

(breath) God spoke creation into being.

(breath) God's word is life.

(breath) God's word accomplishes its purpose.

(breath) God's word fulfills its mission.

(breath) I am created in God's image.

(breath) God's Spirit dwells within me.

(breath) I can speak with God's words.

(breath) When I speak God's words, they have life.

(breath) When I speak God's words, they have God's power.

GOD'S WORD IS LIFE.

DAY 49

Adoration: The Omni-ness of God

Lord, you are great and worthy of the highest praise! For there is no end to the discovery of the greatness that surrounds you.
—PSALM 145:3 (TPT)

A common belief across Christian denominations is the profession of faith in the one living and true God, who is holy and loving, eternal, unlimited in power, wisdom, and goodness. While the exact wording may vary, they all point to the all-ness or, from the Latin, omni-ness of God. Isaiah 46:9 says no one is like God, and 1 Corinthians 15:28 describes Him as all in all or everything in everyone. Here are a few of the commonly expressed omni characteristics of God.

Omnipotent: All-powerful

Omniscient: All-knowing

Omnipresent: Being in all places

Omnisapient: All-wise or wisdom

Omnibenevolent: All good

Omnitemporal: Existing in all time or existing outside of all time

REFLECT

- Is there one characteristic of God that is easier to relate to than the others?
- What characteristic of God would you like to experience in a new way?

Pray

It is difficult for us to comprehend the infiniteness of God. Giving Him worship and praise helps open our minds and hearts to begin to understand Him. Read Psalm 145 as a prayer of praise.

My heart explodes with praise to You! Now and forever my heart bows in worship to You, my King and my God! (Psalm 145:1)

GOD IS ALL IN ALL.

DAY

50

Dedication: My Time

My life, my every moment, my destiny—it's all in your hands.
—PSALM 31:15 (TPT)

The psalmist describes our days on earth like a vapor. Time is limited here. We make time for what we deem necessary and enjoy. I confess, I'm very good at wasting time and can be caught worrying like Martha about the unnecessary details. But our timeless God longs for us to give our moments to Him. I now submit my time to Him through prayer and start the morning like this:

God, You are God, and I am not. You created this day, and I give it to You. Here is my list for today. I give this list over to You and ask You to show me what is on Your list for me today.

When I first shared about this practice with my adult Sunday school class, I was met with shock. I heard, "Are you sure you want to do that? What if He changes your plans? What if He tells you not to go to work? What if

He tells you not to feed your kids, or to go to Africa?" I believe that is the point, to trust in God's "what if."

God has both approved of and redirected my plans. Once, He sent me to the hospital to encourage someone I didn't know. Another time, He took me off my travel route to see and experience His beauty.

REFLECT

- How are you making use of your time?
- Do you surrender your schedule to God?

Pray

God, You hold time in Your hands. I dedicate my time to You. Here is my list for today: _____ (list everything planned). I give this list over to You and ask You to show me what is on Your list for me today. Jesus in me. Amen.

LORD, MY TIME IS YOURS.

DAY

51

Supplication: Wisdom

Wisdom is the most valuable commodity—so buy it!
Revelation-knowledge is what you need—so invest in it!
—PROVERBS 4:7 (TPT)

One of the significant drawbacks of growing up in church and reading the Bible is familiarity with the word. When we feel we already know it, we either don't let it surprise us, miss its depth, or skim it without letting its truth and wisdom wash over us. How does the Holy Spirit draw you into the word? I don't mean how much of the Bible you read daily or whether you read the Bible in a year. Rather, how has the Holy Spirit told you to delight in the word, and are you doing that?

Once when reading from Joel, I was overwhelmed to comprehend the importance of being in God's word. I'd been struggling with the personality and gifts God purposed within one of my daughters. I have a strong right-or-wrong type of personality. If God said it, let's do it and keep at it until we get it right. My lovely daughter is infused with a spring of God's mercy. This spring may overflow and spill out with tears at any second. I had been asking God to give me heavenly wisdom to train her. But I was really looking to make her more like me. Then I read the words of Joel. "Even now," declares the Lord, "return to me with all your heart, with fasting and weeping and mourning" (Joel 2:12 NIV). It took my breath away how God answered the words of my prayer for heavenly wisdom. Thankfully, He didn't grant me the accompanying desire to "make her more like me." I would have missed the heavenly wisdom if I had not been reading God's word.

REFLECT

- Where do your thoughts need a radical transformation to become more like God's thoughts?
- Where do you look for wisdom?

Pray

Holy Father, may I be filled with Your wisdom and Your understanding by Your Spirit that I may comprehend Your will; and as a result, may Your fruit be evident in all that I think, do, and say for Your kingdom to come and Your will to be done here on earth. By the powerful and merciful gift of Jesus Christ, amen.

GOD'S WISDOM IN ME.

DAY 52

Contrition: Repenting on Behalf of My Nation

Give ear, our God, and hear; open your eyes and see the desolation of the city that bears your Name. We do not make requests of you because we are righteous, but because of your great mercy.
—DANIEL 9:18 (NIV)

Continuing the theme introduced on day 46, believers can turn away God's wrath toward their nation by making confessions and repenting on behalf of their country. This concept may be new and uncomfortable. Most of us have been taught that we are responsible for our own sin and that repentance is personal. Daniel, however, provides a different example. His prayers extend beyond himself to include his nation. Daniel prays for his country, and he repents for his sins and the sins of his kings, leaders, ancestors, and country: namely, rebelling and turning away from the Lord (Daniel 9:5, 8–11 NIV).

As believers, we can cry out to the Lord, aligning with the Spirit within and interceding on behalf of the people and leaders of our nation. As we do so, we ask God to pour out His Spirit and awaken the hearts of humanity to receive His love and mercy.

REFLECT

- Do you watch displays of communal sin with detachment?
- Have you considered repenting on behalf of your nation?

Pray

We are quick to ask God to bless our country yet slow to repent on its behalf. The greatest blessing God could lavish on a nation is one of the grace and mercy of His forgiveness: "Also, seek the peace and prosperity of the city to which I have carried you into exile. Pray to the Lord for it, because if it prospers, you too will prosper" (Jeremiah 29:7 NIV).

> *Dear Lord, show me how to pray for my country. My heart weeps over the sins of my nation, and I ask for Your mercy. In Jesus's name, amen.*
>
> *Dear Holy Father, we have sinned. We have been wicked. We have turned away from You. We have hated, and we have destroyed. Lord, Jesus have mercy.*

FORGIVE US, LORD; WE HAVE SINNED.

DAY 53

Spiritual Warfare: Demolishing Strongholds

Our spiritual weapons are energized with divine power to effectively dismantle the defenses behind which people hide.
—2 CORINTHIANS 10:4 (TPT)

Most of our spiritual battle is waged with the protection of putting on the armor of God (Ephesians 6:10). This verse from 2 Corinthians 10, however, is addressing the offensive side of the battle. We cannot tear down the defenses of the evil one without using the offensive weapons available to us. In the "armor of God" passage from Ephesians 6, our offensive weapons include the sword of the spirit, which is the word of God, and prayer.

In order to bring down the defenses of the enemy, we must learn to use the word of God and prayer effectively. The word of God has immense power. It accomplishes the purposes for which it is sent. It was by the word of God that creation came into existence. And God's word has the power to transform our hearts and minds. It is essential to read, pray, and claim God's word. A significant part of praying God's word is to praise God. By declaring praise to the one true God, we tear down thoughts and attitudes that are raised up in defiance of His name (2 Corinthians 10:5). When we release the praise and glory of God's character here on earth, it is released throughout the heavens. Additionally, we use the word of God to forbid or bind up the lies and false doctrine that stand against the truth of God (Matthew 18:18).

REFLECT

- What messages are you writing on your heart?
- Are you speaking and declaring words of love?

Pray

Holy Father, You alone are worthy of all praise. You are God Almighty. You are high and lifted up. Lord, Your word is true, and by Your word, all defenses of the evil one come down. You are perfect love, and through Your word, every deception and every arrogant attitude that opposes You is made captive. Lord, may Your name and Your glory cover the earth as the waters cover the sea, Jesus. Amen.

GOD'S NAME THROUGHOUT THE EARTH.

DAY 54

Standing: Taking Our Post

I will stand at my watch and station myself on the ramparts.
—HABAKKUK 2:1 (NIV)

During especially difficult times, the Lord has led me to the book of Habakkuk, where He revealed to me this prayer strategy of taking my post and standing watch. While we take our post, we stop whining; then we look, stand firm, and watch. This stance is a position of being strong in the Lord. It is a recognition that we do not have the ability to fight difficult battles out of our own strength. As followers of Christ, we stand firm on His promises. We are strengthened in our ability to stand by our trust in the good news of the gospel of Christ and our faith in God. We labor in prayer and intercession, asking God for His good works and His mercy, and then we stand and watch to see what God is doing.

REFLECT

Do you stop in your intercession to see what God is doing?

Pray

Stand and declare that no matter what you face, yet you will praise God.

Heavenly Father, fill me with Your peace; transform my thoughts to think on what is beautiful, what is lovely; lift my eyes to look to You; give me the strength to stand on Your word; close my mouth from uttering words of fear, worry, and rumor. Holy Father, I humbly come before You and ask You to show me Your good works and Your mercy. No matter the storm I face, yet I will praise You and give You glory and honor. By and through the holy name of Jesus. Amen.

I WILL STAND WATCH.

DAY 55

Adoration: More Than . . .

Never doubt God's mighty power to work in you and accomplish all this. He will achieve infinitely more than your greatest request, your most unbelievable dream, and exceed your wildest imagination! He will outdo them all, for his miraculous power constantly energizes you.
—EPHESIANS 3:20 (TPT)

Paul closes his prayer in the third chapter of Ephesians with exuberant declarations of God's ability to do infinitely more than we request. He can exceed our wildest imaginations. So often, we limit God by not even coming to Him with our requests. When my husband and I began the process of answering the Lord's call to add children to our family through the foster care system, we were required to go through many hours of training. In one of the classes, the instructor talked of common traumas that children within the foster care system experience. Additionally, she explained the various lingering physical, mental, and spiritual impacts resulting from the initial ordeals. During the class, I became overwhelmed with the realization that I was not enough. I silently prayed, *God, I am not enough for all this. Are You?* His answer enveloped my whole being: *I am more than.*

REFLECT

- Have you put God inside a box of limited expectations?
- What have you not asked of God?

Pray

One way to allow God to burst open the walls of the box of our set limitations is to praise Him for being more than. Use Psalm 40:5 as the starting place for your adoration of God.

O Lord, our God, no one can compare with you. Such wonderful works and miracles are all found with you! And you think of us all the time with your countless expressions of love—far exceeding our expectations! (Psalm 40:5)

GOD, YOU ARE MORE THAN.

DAY
56

Dedication: Trust

Blessing after blessing comes to those who love and trust the Lord. They will not fall away, for they refuse to listen to the lies of the proud.
—PSALM 40:4 (TPT)

I'm not one for New Year's resolutions, but going into a new year once, the Lord nudged me to focus on the word "trust" for the upcoming year. I began that year with high hopes. However, it all quickly crashed down. This year of trust involved physical and mental illness, breakdowns in relationships, and my stroke. How could there be truth to Psalm 40:4, of blessings coming to those who trust the Lord? I had to surrender my understanding of, and dedicate, my trust to the Lord.

As I questioned Him, God gave me a word for each letter of "trust": "timeless," "resource," "U-turn," "surprise," and "tree." Timeless, the Lord holds all of time in His hands. He calls us to release time-limited goals and dwell with Him in the moment. God is the resource for us and our hopes. "U-turn" commands we change direction toward the Lord. When we make this U-turn, we discover that He is always right there. Then, with our eyes on Him, He surprises us with His love. He is the tree of life, and all life is in Him. As part of my stroke recovery, I began to draw. One day, I showed my sketches to a friend, saying, "And here is a dead tree." To this, she responded, "No, this is a tree full of the potential of new life." The Lord gives us the seasons as a promise of His new life.

REFLECT

- What is your definition of trust in the Lord?
- What are the blessings of trusting in the Lord?

Pray

Our response to the chaos surrounding us must be to let go of our false sense of control and to put our times in the hands of our sovereign Father, the One who knows our soul.

Heavenly Father, I trust in You. I commit my spirit into Your hand. I release my times and this situation (name your times, your concerns) into Your hands. Strengthen my heart as I hope in You. Jesus, fill me with Your hope. Amen.

I TRUST IN GOD.

DAY

57

Supplication: Healing

Are there any believers in your fellowship suffering great hardship and distress? Encourage them to pray! Are there happy, cheerful ones among you? Encourage them to sing out their praises! Are there any sick among you? Then ask the elders of the church to come and pray over the sick and anoint them with oil in the name of our Lord.
—JAMES 5:13–14 (TPT)

Scripture does not command us to search out God's subjective will concerning healing, but it does command us to ask for healing. If we do not ask for healing, we make no room for God to heal. I have been used of God to bring healing in others, and I have received the miracle of God's healing touch.

At a conference on healing prayer, the speaker asked, "What ailment are you just living with?" He went on to say that we shouldn't call it our "thorn of the flesh" until we have unceasingly prayed for God to heal it. After the conference, I started praying about my feet. Due to an injury, my left foot was significantly smaller than my right. So much so, I had to buy two different pairs of shoes. I started each morning claiming healing for my feet, saying the many promises of scripture about feet. I continued this for 40 days. On day 41, I sat with my feet together, and I almost didn't even notice they were the same size. But then the reality of it sank in. They were the same size! The Lord had restored my feet.

REFLECT

- Do you pray for your own healing?
- Do you pray for God to heal others?

Pray

God, You are the God that heals me. I praise You for the mighty work of healing of _____. Father, I ask that You breathe Your breath of life in and through me and heal _____. In the name of Jesus, amen.
    By the authority given to me from Christ Jesus, _____ be healed. Amen.

HEALING OF THE LORD UPON _____.

DAY 58

Contrition: Seventy Times Seven

> *Later Peter approached Jesus and said, "How many times do I have to forgive my fellow believer who keeps offending me? Seven times?" Jesus answered, "Not seven times, Peter, but seventy times seven times!*
> —MATTHEW 18:21–22 (TPT)

As people, we tend to keep score in just about everything. It is even difficult for us to enjoy the beauty of God's creation without giving it some numerical score. Peter seems to be a scorekeeper as well. He wants to know just how many times he must forgive. I feel almost sure that he considers his offer of seven times is more than extortionate. And yet, Jesus sets the goal even higher. Seventy times seven is the response. I have done the math; this is 490 times. If this number were the goal, it still would not be possible to achieve without the mercy of Jesus freely flowing through us. However, the answer is not in the number. It is the heart behind the number. Jesus is calling us to live a lifestyle of mercy and forgiveness. Additionally,

He teaches that the world will know the truth of who He is by how they see us loving other believers.

While God declares He forgets, in our humanity, forgiveness does not mean we have forgotten. Forgiveness allows us to see the other person how God sees them and grants us freedom from the pain and bondage associated with the memories. When we repent to God, we ask Him to see us for who we are today and not remember our former selves. Likewise, when we offer forgiveness, we choose to believe the best in that person and that they have a changed heart.

REFLECT

- If God kept a record of your wrongs, how many would He score against you?
- Have you ever refused to forgive someone when you were asked?

Pray

The gift of mercy and forgiveness in our relationships aligns our behavior and our heart with the word of God.

Heavenly Father, I release my pain and the pieces of my heart to You. Open my heart to allow Your mercy to flow through me to _____. Through the love and compassion of Jesus, amen.

LIVING MERCY FLOW THROUGH ME.

DAY 59

Spiritual Warfare: Claiming Gates

So wake up, you living gateways, and rejoice! Fling wide, you eternal doors! Here he comes; the King of Glory is ready to come in.
—PSALM 24:9 (TPT)

Kingdom gate claiming is physically praying, interceding, and planting the kingdom flag in the ground for Jesus Christ. It's walking the land, desiring to see it as God does. Joshua and Caleb exemplify this walking throughout the Promised Land. There were giants in the land and cities with great walls, but Joshua and Caleb believed that God would lead and protect them (Numbers 14:8b,9b). Throughout history, to control the gates of one's enemies was to conquer their city. Part of Abraham's blessing from the Lord was the promise that his "offspring shall possess the gate of his enemies" (Genesis 22:17). As children of God, we are called to aid the redemption of the land, so that God's kingdom will come and His will shall be done here on earth as in heaven.

What are today's gates? Gates are any penetrations into our communities, homes, and lives. They can be physical openings, such as doors, borders, and airports. Additionally, they can be openings for knowledge and information, such as education, TV, and the internet. We want to protect both the doorways into our lives and the doorways for ministry: "There's an amazing door of opportunity standing wide open for me to minister here, even though there are many who oppose and stand against me" (1 Corinthians 16:9).

REFLECT

- What are some open gates in your community, home, and life?
- What is significant about claiming these gates for the Lord?

Pray

Gate claiming involves taking our prayers and our intercessions to the very places where we desire to see God's presence manifested and our prayers of redemption and transformation answered.

Lord, I pray that You will send down the river of the water of life from Your throne room over this gate _____ (name the opening). May Your river come crashing down like a mighty waterfall and cleanse this gate and claim it for You, the King of Glory. For the name of the glory of the Lord Jesus, amen.

GATES FOR THE KING OF GLORY.

DAY

60

Resting: It Is Good

Now I can say to myself and to all, "Relax and rest, be confident and serene, for the Lord rewards fully those who simply trust in him."
—PSALM 116:7 (TPT)

As an example, God rested. Was the Creator of the Universe tired? I do not believe that in creating all things God experienced tiredness as we understand it. Yet He stopped, enjoyed the fruit of His creation, and rested. When the disciples returned to Jesus and reported to Him all that they had done, Jesus called them to come away with Him and rest. This rest is a time of "not doing" with Jesus.

In the world, we labor. We spend time working, learning, and ministering. Much of what we are doing is good. Still, God makes provision for us to enter into His rest. In the Old Testament, when the Lord talks about rest, He always makes provision for it. With the manna from heaven, there was always enough to last two days. And it was given on the day before the Sabbath. When He calls Israel to provide the land with a Sabbath rest the next year, it produces enough for both the current and the following year. A significant part of entering into the Lord's rest is trusting Him to provide. Psalm 116 opens with "I am passionately in love with God because he listens to me. He hears my prayers and answers them. As long as I live I'll keep praying to him, for he stoops down to listen to my heart's cry." And it is out of this relationship with God that we trust Him enough to rest in Him.

REFLECT

- How do you rest?
- How is God calling you to rest in Him?

Pray

Today, find your desolate place—a place without entertainment or electronic disruptions. Maybe light a candle as a symbol and join in God's holy rest.

Lord Jesus Christ, open my ears to hear You call me to rest with You. Burden my soul with the desire to withdraw to a desolate place with You and receive Your rest. Amen.

RECEIVE GOD'S REST.

A FINAL WORD

✦

We decided to take a tour canoeing down the "River of Golden Dreams" on a family vacation. Loaded up in our canoes and kayaks, we began our journey across the lake to the mouth of the river. After entering the river, a reality unfolded that was much different than the name led us to believe.

This so-called River of Golden Dreams was more of a drainage ditch flowing beside a railroad track. We spent much of our time with our heads down and our backs straining against the paddles. We labored on our journey, trying to navigate the waterway curves without slamming against the thick trees and brush growing along the banks.

Then there were brief moments when the stream would open, the current would slow, and we were able to lift our eyes to the beautiful mountain vistas that surrounded us. It was, of course, these moments that we captured and posted on social media. And I am sure these are the moments that gave this journey its name.

Our relationship with God is similar to my experience on the River of Golden Dreams. We begin excited about meeting with Him, full of hopes of mountaintop experiences. And somewhere along the path, we find ourselves toiling in the mundane, wondering where we are and what we are doing.

It is an abiding relationship with Christ that launches believers into the dimensions where God sovereignly works in the affairs of humanity. We are welcomed into this relationship by the Lord Himself, and the Lord's prayer provides us a structure for our relationship with God.

I hope that as you journeyed through these 10 cycles of the petitions of the Lord's Prayer, you have seen and learned that God loves to commune with you, and that He welcomes you to converse with Him from your whole heart.

REFERENCES

Biblehub. "Lamentations 3:24." Accessed July 8, 2021. BibleHub.com/lamentations/3-24.htm#lexicon.

Boswell, James. *Healing Broken and Damaged Relationships*. Discipleship Training Center. 2000.

Chambers, Oswald. *My Utmost for His Highest: The Golden Book of Oswald Chambers (Selections for the Year)*. New York: Dodd, Mead & Company, 1935.

Foster, Richard J. *Prayer: Finding the Heart's True Home (10th Anniversary Edition)*. New York: HarperCollins, 2009.

Gallup. "Religion." Gallup.com. Accessed June 24, 2021. News.Gallup.com/poll/1690/religion.aspx.

Geringer, Sarah. *Transforming Your Thought Life: Christian Meditation in Focus*. Abilene, TX: Leafwood Publishers, 2019.

Goll, James W. *Praying with God's Heart: The Power and Purpose of Prophetic Intercession*. Minneapolis, MN: Baker Publishing Group, 2018.

Lexico. "Majesty." Accessed September 3, 2021. Lexico.com/definition/majesty.

Mullins, Rich. "Boy Like Me/Man Like You." Track 2 on *The World as Best as I Remember It, Volume One*. Reunion Records, 1991.

National Day of Prayer Task Force. "Willing and Doing His Good Pleasure." May 5, 2021. Accessed June 23, 2021. NationalDayOfPrayer.org/willing_and_doing_his_good_pleasure.

Reininger, Gustave, and Thomas Keating. *Centering Prayer in Daily Life and Ministry*. New York: Continuum International Publishing Group Ltd., 1998.

Russell, Corey. *Pursuit of the Holy*. Kansas City, MO: Forerunner Publishing, 2006.

Ryle, John Charles. *Expository Thoughts on the Gospels: St. John, Volume 3*. London: Banner of Truth Trust, 2012.

Tada, J. *Living Beyond Life's Circumstances*. Brentwood, TN: Integrity Publishers, 2003.

Therkelsen, Margaret. *The Love Exchange: An Adventure in Prayer*. Eugene, OR: Wipf and Stock Publishers, 2003.

TobyMac. "Move (Keep Walkin') - Live." Track 10 on *Hits Deep Live*. ForeFront Records, 2016.

Torrison, Rick. "The Power of a Posture Video Series." YouTube. July 27, 2021. Video, 6:36. YouTube.com/watch?v=dz7SzeVgIp0.

UPPERROOM. "Surrounded (Fight My Battles)." Capitol CMG, August 21, 2018. Video, 10:41. YouTube.com/watch?v=vx6mfAgHDsY.

Walt, J. D. "The Second Half of the Gospel: The Ten Transformational Stops." SeedBed. August 9, 2021. SeedBed.com/the-second-half-of-the-gospel-the-ten-transformational-stops

ACKNOWLEDGMENTS

✸

In developing this book, I am forever grateful to my mom, Diane Swalin, who was my first prayer teacher, and for the loving encouragement of my husband, Tom. I give a special thanks to all my family and friends who served as prayer warriors and assisted me through rehab and recovery. And of course, Annie, my dog sent by God to wake me up the night of my stroke.

ABOUT THE AUTHOR

✸

Filled with the passion for leading others into living the prayer-filled life, Elaine Goddard serves the body of Christ as a personal prayer trainer, biblical intercessor, and Christian life coach. Formerly with NASA, Elaine answered the Lord's call out of rocket science and outer space to focus on inner space by writing and speaking on deepening our relationship with God through prayer and inner healing. She currently serves as a lay prayer leader at Friendswood United Methodist Church and writes at Highway2Him.com.

CPSIA information can be obtained
at www.ICGtesting.com
Printed in the USA
JSHW042340291121
20849JS00008B/10

9 781638 070764